D1499307

INCOME TAX EXEMPTIONS

INCOME TAX EXEMPTIONS

AN ANALYSIS OF THE EFFECTS OF PERSONAL EXEMPTIONS ON THE INCOME TAX STRUCTURE

BY

MICHAEL E. LEVY

Division of Economic Studies,
National Industrial Conference Board, New York

1960

NORTH-HOLLAND PUBLISHING COMPANY-AMSTERDAM

PRINTED IN THE NETHERLANDS

PREFACE

This book is an outgrowth of an earlier study submitted as a doctoral dissertation at Columbia University. Over the past two years, the original manuscript has undergone a moderate expansion and substantial revisions and re-organizations. However, I have not attempted to modify the basic approach which is predominantly "analytical" rather than "institutional." It is hardly necessary to spell out the particular advantages or limitations of such an approach.

While the present study is addressed primarily to the specialist in the field, it also contains a good deal of material which is likely to be of interest to the general economist or even the student of economics. This is particularly true with regard to Chapters I and V. Chapters III and IV, Section D, may also fall into this category, even though this material is a good deal more intricate.

I am grateful to the Department of Economics, Columbia University, for a fellowship in 1955 without which this study might never have gotten off the ground. I am indebted to many persons who have read earlier versions of this book and whose valuable comments have resulted in substantial improvements. Most of all, I am deeply grateful to Professor Carl S. Shoup for his penetrating criticism and continuous encouragement. Without his sustained interest this book would never have been published.

I am also very much indebted to Professors William Vickrey, Arthur F. Burns, C. Lowell Harriss, and Abba P. Lerner for comments which greatly benefited this study, even though I could not always do full justice to them. Additional valuable criticism was contributed by members of the Economic Research Center in Public Finance, Columbia University, who were subjected to an earlier version of Chapters I and IV.

I would like to thank the Economic Research Center of Columbia University for the provision of funds which enabled me to avail myself of the services of a trained mathematician, Mr. Gideon Schwarz, for the editing and streamlining of my Mathematical Appendices. Indeed, Mr. Schwarz's work went far beyond this. Not only did he succeed in improving the conciseness and elegance of formulation of the Appendices but, in addition, he was able to develop each Appendix into an independent, readable unit.

Needless to say, I am fully responsible for whatever flaws and shortcomings may be contained in this study and the ideas expressed therein do not necessarily reflect the views of any of the organizations with which I have been affiliated in the past or present.

New York   MICHAEL E. LEVY
November 4, 1959

TABLE OF CONTENTS

LIST OF TABLES

LIST OF ILLUSTRATIONS

I. FIGURES

II. PLATES

INTRODUCTION

The purpose of this study is to provide an extensive and systematic analysis of income tax exemptions and tax rate changes with special emphasis on the impact on the average rate, the degree of tax progressivity, and incentives to work. General economic theory is applied to specific features of income taxation in order to derive broad generalizations of wide applicability without either getting lost in the rich variety of institutional detail or becoming entangled in non-economic normative problems.[1]

To my knowledge, there exists no such comprehensive analysis; moreover, some parts of the present study deal with questions which have been explored only in a very cursory fashion or not at all. This is especially true with regard to the choice and application of "tax criteria," the analysis of the vanishing exemption and the transformation of a progressive tax with a linearly declining exemption into one with a continuing exemption (Chapter I); also with regard to the classification and analysis of "fundamental" rate changes by type of rate change (Chapter III), the treatment of statutory revenue changes in relation to incentives to work (Chapter IV), and the discussion of tax credits (Chapter V).

However, this should by no means imply that the present study covers an area which is almost completely "terra incognita." Much work had been done previously, even if most of it is rather diffused and scattered. For general orientation, it may be helpful to present, at the outset, a brief outline of the logical order and sequence of the present study together with those bibliographical references which contain the most interesting and relevant work previously done.

---

[1] Of course, many generalizations may prove extremely helpful in providing the basis for normative judgments of given alternatives.

Needless to say, my own indebtedness is great in each and every case.

At the outset of Chapter I, the three basic types of exemption (initial, vanishing, and continuing) are defined. Then, a set of "tax criteria" is developed, that is, a set of limitations is placed on the income tax function in accordance with what, at present, is considered a well-constructed and equitable tax. Finally, the tax criteria are applied to the basic types of exemption. It is found that some types of exemption can be ruled out as inconsistent with the tax criteria. In this connection, Professor Pigou's pioneering discussion of income tax criteria has been of great value.[2]

In Chapter II, the linearly declining and continuing exemptions are analyzed with regard to their absolute and relative value to the taxpayer under proportional taxation and their impact on the average tax rate and on tax progressivity. Thereafter, changes in the parameters of the proportional tax (that is, changes in the rate of decline of the exemption, the proportional tax rate, and the maximum size of the exemption) are considered. Some of this material has been treated by KARL BRÄUER in his "Umrisse und Untersuchungen zu einer Lehre vom Steuertarif."[3]

The discussion in Chapter II sets the stage for the more complex analysis of the continuing exemption under progressive taxation in Chapter III. Of particular interest in this chapter are Sections D and E. In Section D, the progressive tax is transformed into a series of proportional tax-bands with (bracket-)exemptions. This device, which greatly facilitates the analysis, has been employed previously by PIERRE FOLLIET in his interesting book "Les tarifs d'impôts."[4] Section E classifies "fundamental" rate changes into three basic types, leading to interesting generalizations with regard to the impact on the average tax rate and on tax progressivity.

In Chapter III, graphic presentation is employed even more

[2] A. C. PIGOU, *A Study in Public Finance* (3d revised ed.; London: Macmillan & Co., Ltd., 1947), Pt. II, Chap. 2.

[3] KARL BRÄUER, *Umrisse und Untersuchungen zu einer Lehre vom Steuertarif* (Jena: Gustave Fischer, 1927), esp. pp. 74–91.

[4] PIERRE FOLLIET, *Les Tarifs d'Impôts; Essai de Mathématiques Fiscales* (Lausanne: Librairie Payot, 1947), § 34.

extensively than elsewhere. Surprisingly, the graphic presentation and analysis, so well-entrenched in the United States, has made little headway in the field of taxation. Here, again, I am particularly indebted to the stimulating graphs in Folliet's book.[5]

Chapter IV draws extensively on the tools and generalizations of the earlier chapters in order to analyze statutory revenue changes. Here, the two basic alternatives of rate changes versus changes in the size of the exemptions are compared.[6] The most original and important material in this chapter is contained in Section D which deals with incentives to work in a somewhat novel way.[7]

Finally, Chapter V completes the present study with an analysis of the two major types of "quasi-exemption," the tax credit and the "standard deduction."

A few comments about the Mathematical Appendices may be in order. The purpose of these Appendices is to provide a concise mathematical treatment and proofs for important, but rather complex, material in the text which deserves more than a cursory mathematical footnote. The Mathematical Appendices run parallel to the text. Nevertheless, an attempt has been made to make them as autonomous and readable as possible in and of themselves.

---

[5] Plates V–VIII are adaptations of Folliet's "Graphique 13" (FOLLIET, *op. cit.*,). Moreover, the use of "original" graphs in the present study was also greatly stimulated by Folliet's illuminating use of "graphiques."

[6] Professor Vickrey has done some interesting work on this topic; see esp. WILLIAM VICKREY, "Adjustment of Income Tax Schedules for Small Incomes," in *Federal Tax Policy for Economic Growth and Stability*, Papers Submitted by Panelists Appearing Before the Subcommittee on Tax Policy; Joint Committee on the Economic Report (U.S. Government Printing Office; Washington, 1956), pp. 347–353; also WILLIAM VICKREY, "Rate Reduction or Increased Exemptions," National Tax Association, *1954 Proceedings of the Forty-seventh Annual Conference on Taxation* (Sacramento, California: 1955), pp. 288–295.

[7] There exists a very extensive literature on incentives to work. A selection of some of the most important discussions of incentive effects is listed at the beginning of Section D, in Chapter IV.

CHAPTER I

THE EXEMPTIONS AND TAX CRITERIA
FOR INCOME TAXATION

At the outset of this chapter, the three basic types of exemption under consideration will be defined and their basic similarities and differences made explicit. Thereafter, a set of limitations on the income tax function termed "tax criteria" will be put forth which should be met by the income tax in general, and by the exemption in particular, in order to make the tax generally acceptable. Finally, the conditions will be established under which the various types of exemption are consistent with this set of "tax criteria."

A. Types of Income Tax Exemption

There exist three basic types of income tax exemption all of which represent a reduction of "net income"[1] by a certain amount in order to derive "taxable income."[2] The basic difference between the three types of exemption lies in the exact relationship between the size of income and the size of the exemption. We shall label the three types of exemption: (1) initial exemption, (2) vanishing exemption, and (3) continuing exemption.[3]

---

[1] Hereafter, the term "net income" will be used as referring to that part of total income to which the tax rates would be directly applied in absence of an exemption, i.e., the term refers to income after deduction of all business and non-business deductions, except exemptions, which are granted by the tax laws (henceforth, quotation marks will be omitted).

[2] Hereafter, the term "taxable income" will be used as referring to that part of total income to which the tax rates are directly applied, i.e., to income net of all permissible deductions and exemptions. Thus "taxable income" = "net income"-exemptions (henceforth, quotation marks will be omitted).

[3] See WILLIAM J. SHULTZ AND C. LOWELL HARRISS, *American Public Finance* (7th ed.; Englewood Cliffs, N. J.: Prentice-Hall, Inc., 1959), p. 192. The authors

1. INITIAL EXEMPTIONS

The initial exemption is defined as the complete exemption from tax liability of net income up to a certain level, beyond which net income (including the amount which was initially exempted) is fully taxable.

2. VANISHING EXEMPTIONS

The vanishing exemption is defined as the complete exemption from tax liability of net income up to a certain level, beyond which the amount deducted from net income in order to derive taxable income declines as net income increases, until the exemption vanishes.

This decline in the size of the exemption can be achieved in many ways. One common device is the reduction by steps. This is illustrated by the solid lines in Figure 1.a. The undesirability of this device is clearly demonstrated by the vertical jumps in taxable income. A critical analysis will be found in Section C of this chapter. (Actually, the "initial exemption" is best viewed as a special case of this type of exemption, that is, an exemption which declines by one single step.)

Some countries, realizing the defect of these "jumps," have let the exemption vanish in a fairly smooth, more or less continuous, way. Such systems can be found mainly in some countries of the British Commonwealth.[4] This has been achieved by increasing the number of steps and reducing the height of the "jumps" until (in the limiting case) a continuous, linear decline will result (see broken line in Figure 1.a). The same result can be achieved by a simple mathematical formula (see § 4 of this section). According to the slope of the line of decline, the exemption will decline at a faster (slower)

---

call the first type "lump-sum exemption." Professor SHOUP has suggested the more descriptive term "initial exemption" which seems preferable to me. For a mathematical statement of the three types of exemption, see *Mathematical Appendix* to Chapter I.

[4] E.g., see KARL BRÄUER, *Umrisse und Untersuchungen zu einer Lehre vom Steuertarif* (Jena: Gustav Fischer, 1927), pp. 88–89.

rate over a smaller (larger) range of net income.[5] Of course, the exemption could also decline in a curvilinear pattern. For the sake of simplicity, we shall restrict ourselves to the analysis of linearly declining exemptions.

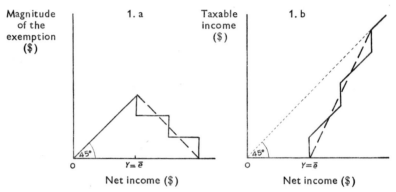

Fig. 1. Exemption declining by steps and linearly declining exemption

Notes:
    The "magnitude of the exemption" at any given net income level is the amount that is deducted from net income in order to derive taxable income.
    $\bar{e}$ denotes the "maximum exemption," that is, the maximum amount of net income which is tax exempt.

3. CONTINUING EXEMPTIONS

The continuing exemption is defined as the complete exemption from tax liability of net income up to a certain level, beyond which taxable income is the amount by which net income exceeds this maximum exemption.

4. RELATION BETWEEN THE THREE TYPES OF EXEMPTION

All three types of exemption have in common the complete exemption from tax liability of net income up to a certain level, called the maximum exemption ($\bar{e}$). Beyond this level, the basic difference lies in the different rates and ranges of decline of the

---

    [5] For a more explicit treatment see § 4 of this chapter.

exemption. The rate of decline of the exemption is instantaneously infinite (and zero thereafter) for the initial exemption and alternatingly instantaneously infinite and zero for an exemption declining by steps. For the linearly declining exemption it is constant (between zero and infinity) over the range of the linear decline— and zero thereafter. Finally, for the continuing exemption it is zero throughout. This relationship between the various types of exemption is best visualized when the exemption $e(Y)$ (for net income levels in excess of the maximum exemption ($\bar{e}$)) is defined as a function of net income in the following way:

(1) $\quad e(Y) = \bar{e} - k(Y - \bar{e})$ for the range of Y, $\bar{e} \leq Y \leq \bar{e} + \dfrac{\bar{e}}{k}$;

(2) $\quad e(Y) = 0$ $\qquad\qquad$ for the range of Y, $\qquad Y \geq \bar{e} + \dfrac{\bar{e}}{k}$;

where Y represents net income and k represents the rate of decline

TABLE 1. *Relation between the rate of decline of the exemption (k) and the range over which the exemption declines ($\bar{e}/k$)*

Rate of decline of the exemp- tion (k)	Net income level at which the exemption vanishes $(Y = \bar{e} + \bar{e}/k)$		Net income range over which the exemption declines $(\bar{e}/k)$	
	in units of $\bar{e}$	in dollars for $\bar{e} = \$600$	in units of $\bar{e}$	in dollars for $\bar{e} = \$600$
(1)	(2)	(3)	(4)	(5)
→0[a]	$\infty\,\bar{e}$	∞	$\infty\,\bar{e}$	∞
0.05	$21.00\bar{e}$	12,600	$20.00\bar{e}$	12,000
0.10	$11.00\bar{e}$	6,600	$10.00\bar{e}$	6,000
0.25	$5.00\bar{e}$	3,000	$4.00\bar{e}$	2,400
0.50	$3.00\bar{e}$	1,800	$2.00\bar{e}$	1,200
1.00	$2.00\bar{e}$	1,200	$1.00\bar{e}$	600
2.00	$1.50\bar{e}$	900	$0.50\bar{e}$	300
10.00	$1.10\bar{e}$	660	$0.10\bar{e}$	60
100.00	$1.01\bar{e}$	606	$0.01\bar{e}$	6
→∞[b]	$1.00\bar{e}$	600	0	0

[a] Limiting case: continuing exemption.
[b] Limiting case: initial exemption.
Note:
$\quad$ Y denotes net income, $\bar{e}$ denotes the maximum exemption.

of the exemption as a function of net income. The meaning and effect of k are illustrated in Table 1 and in Figure 2. For example, for $k = 0.05$ (Table 1, line 2), an increase in net income of one dollar reduces the exemption by five cents for net income levels between $\bar{e}$ and $21\bar{e}$. Given the maximum exemption $\bar{e} = \$600$, the exemption will vanish at the net income level of $\$12,600$, that is, it will decline over a range of $\$12,000$. For $k = 2.00$ (Table 1, line 7), an increase in net income of one dollar reduces the exemption by two dollars for net income levels between $\bar{e}$ and $1.50\bar{e}$. Therefore, given the maximum exemption $\bar{e} = \$600$, the exemption will vanish at the net income level of $\$900$, that is, it will decline over a range of $\$300$.

In general, the greater the rate of decline of the exemption, the smaller the range over which the exemption declines. Therefore, the

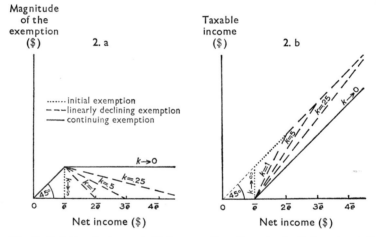

Fig. 2. Relation between initial exemption, linearly declining exemption, and continuing exemption

Notes:

The "magnitude of the exemption" at any given net income level (Y) is the amount $(e(Y))$ that is deducted from net income in order to derive taxable income.

$\bar{e}$ denotes the "maximum exemption," that is, the maximum amount of net income which is tax exempt.

k denotes the rate of decline of the exemption; the exemption, over its range of decline, being defined by the function:

$$\bar{e}(Y) = \bar{e} - k(Y - \bar{e}) \qquad \text{for} \qquad \bar{e} \leq Y \leq \bar{e} + \frac{\bar{e}}{k}.$$

continuing exemption ($k \to 0$) and the initial exemption ($k \to \infty$) can both be viewed as limiting cases of the linearly declining exemption ($0 < k < \infty$).

Figure 2 presents graphically the effect of the rate of decline of the exemption on the magnitude of the exemption (2.a) and on taxable income (2.b).

The preceding analysis stressed the common elements of the three basic types of exemption. It would, however, be quite misleading to conclude that the differences among these three types of exemption are slight and unimportant. That these differences are crucial, will become clearer after a short digression on the nature and characteristics of properly designed income tax functions which provides some criteria for evaluating the appropriateness of various forms of income tax exemptions.

B. The Nature of the Income Tax Function and the Tax Criteria

The income tax function, or functional relationship between total income tax liability and total income[6] of a tax-paying unit during a specified time interval,[7] is best visualized by means of a co-ordinate system where the total tax liability $f(Y)$ is measured along the vertical axis and total income (Y) along the horizontal axis, with the relevant time dimension explicitly stated (see Figure 3). To begin with, any tax function (that is, any relationship which assigns to each value of Y one, and only one, value of $f(Y)$) may be considered. Hence, conditions have to be imposed which restrict the shape of the tax function and the area within which it may fall. There exists, at best, one single "objective" condition which serves this purpose. The tax liability should not exceed "ability to pay;" otherwise the

---

[6] A large number of different income concepts can be used to define the tax function. Throughout our analysis, the question of the most appropriate income concept for tax purposes is eliminated from the discussion and "net income" (as defined in section A of this chapter) is used as the basic income concept to which the tax liability is related.

[7] In most countries, one year is the basic time unit with regard to which the tax liability is defined. Some fundamental problems connected with the time dimension of the income tax will be briefly discussed at the end of this section.

tax becomes a self-defeating measure.[8] Of course, "ability to pay" is open to several interpretations which introduce "subjective" elements. A broad interpretation would limit total income tax liability to an amount equal to, or smaller than, total (positive) income.[9] As a result, three eighth of the area of our co-ordinate

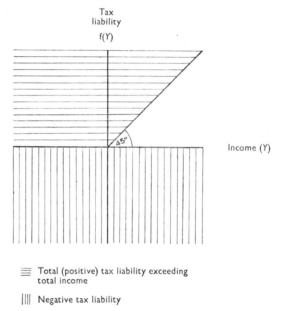

$\equiv$ Total (positive) tax liability exceeding total income

||| Negative tax liability

Fig. 3. Restriction of the income tax function to positive tax liabilities not exceeding total income over time period t

system are eliminated as "inadmissible" (the entire second quadrant and that half of the first quadrant which lies above the forty-five

---

[8] For a summary discussion of "objective" and "subjective" factors affecting "ability to pay," see WILHELM GERLOFF, "Steuerwirtschaftslehre," in *Handbuch der Finanzwissenschaft*, II (2nd ed.; Tübingen: J. C. B. Mohr (Paul Siebeck), 1956), pp. 281–285.

[9] One may argue that the tax liability should fall short of the "minimum subsistence" income. However, the notion of "minimum subsistence" is too vague to serve as a useful, quasi-objective guidance. Also, the existence of wealth may extend "ability to pay" beyond the level of current income, at least temporarily. From a purely operational point of view, the interpretation used in the text is probably the most useful one.

degree line through the origin), as indicated by the horizontally shaded area in Figure 3. Another half—the vertically shade area—can be eliminated if negative tax liabilities are ruled out.[10] The remaining task is not so much one of further limiting the area within which the income tax function may fall, but rather one of restricting the shape of the function. Here, one has to rely on purely subjective conditions, that is, value judgments.[11] One of the first economists to clearly spell out such a set of restricting conditions was Professor PIGOU.[12] At this point, it may be fruitful to list Pigou's four conditions, or tax criteria, and to discuss them critically. It will then be possible to modify them in order to derive a set of somewhat more restrictive tax criteria which will better characterize those types of income tax which are considered generally acceptable and properly designed at present.

PIGOU proposes that (1) the tax levy on nil income should be nil; (2) the amount assessed on a smaller income should not exceed the amount assessed on a larger income; (3) the average rate of taxation should not increase for some increases in the amount of income while decreasing for other increases; and (4) the total amount of the tax levy should never exceed the amount of the income on which it is levied.[13] If the tax function is denoted by $R = f(Y)$, where R is the tax liability of the taxpayer, and Y the amount of his income, Pigou's four conditions can be expressed thus:

(1) $$f(0) = 0.$$

---

[10] Indeed, there exists no valid reason for ruling out negative tax liabilities, that is, tax refunds, subsidies, deficiency payments, and the like. However, these can be dealt with either by such devices as "loss carry-over" or income averaging, or by considering them positive government expenditures rather than negative tax receipts.

[11] The tendency of modern economists to keep aloof from value judgments accounts to a large extent for the general neglect of this area of enquiry.

[12] A. C. PIGOU, *A Study in Public Finance* (1st ed.; London: Macmillan and Co., Ltd., 1928), Pt. II, Chap. 2; (3d (revised)) ed.; London: Macmillan and Co., Ltd., 1947), Pt. II, Chap. 2. The text of this chapter is virtually unchanged in the third (revised) edition. This latter edition is used for all further references.

[13] *Ibid.*, p. 47.

(2) $$f'(Y) \geqq 0$$

for all values of Y.[14]

(3)
$$\frac{d\,\dfrac{f(Y)}{Y}}{dY}$$

must consistently be positive—or consistently negative—for all values of Y.[14]

(4) $$f(Y) \leqq Y$$

for all values of Y.

Pigou's first tax criterion requires that the tax function pass through the origin of the co-ordinates. At present, it is generally agreed that the income tax should provide for some exemption, even if only for the purely administrative reason that the revenue collected from the taxpayer should exceed the cost of collection.[15] Hence, the following modification seems appropriate:

TAX CRITERION I: THE TAX LEVY ON AN INCOME LESS THAN, OR EQUAL TO, A SPECIFIC AMOUNT (EXEMPTION) SHALL BE ZERO[16]

Pigou's second tax criterion states that the marginal rate shall be greater than (or equal to) zero for all income levels. This condition permits a marginal rate structure in which the marginal rate increases for some increases in income while decreasing for other increases (for example, see Table 2, cols. 1 and 2). This type of marginal rate scale is not excluded even when Pigou's third condition is added in its progressive form, that is, if the average rate increases throughout

---

[14] This formulation implies that $f(Y)$ is differentiable throughout which need not be the case. Our treatment simply follows PIGOU, *op. cit.*, p. 47. For a generalized treatment, see *Mathematical Appendix* to Chapter I.

[15] Needless to say, this is by no means the only, or even the most compelling, argument in favor of an income tax exemption. The notion of a tax-free "subsistence level" is hundreds of years old (see DOPSCH, as quoted by GERLOFF, *loc. cit.*, p. 282). In recent times, it has also been suggested that an income tax exemption is necessary in order to counteract and correct the regressive incidence of the indirect taxes at the bottom of the income distribution.

[16] Pigou's condition is merely the special and limiting case where the "specific amount" is zero.

as income increases.[17] Thus, Pigou's conditions permit an income tax which is uniformly progressive, when progressivity is measured by the rate of change of the average rate, while being regressive over part of the income range, when progressivity is measured by the rate of change of the marginal rate.[18] To be sure, Professor PIGOU asserts that such an inconsistency is ruled out by his third condition; he even provides what he considers a proof of this assertion.[19] However, all he actually proves is that such an inconsistency is ruled out if and only if the marginal rate increases throughout, as income

TABLE 2. *Example of an income tax which fulfills all four of Pigou's conditions and which is progressive throughout, when progressivity is measured by the rate of change of the average rate, but alternatingly progressive-regressive, when progressivity is measured by the rate of change of the marginal rate*

Income range ($) (1)	Marginal rate (2)	Rate of change of marginal rate[a] (3)	Total income[b] ($) (4)	Tax liability[b] ($) (5)	Average rate (6)	Rate of change of average rate[a] (7)
0–1000	.05		1000	50	.05	
		.20				.10
1000–2000	.25		2000	300	.15	
		—.04				.02
2000–3000	.21		3000	510	.17	
		.08				.03
3000–4000	.29		4000	800	.20	
		—.04				.01
4000–5000	.25		5000	1050	.21	
		.08				.02
5000–6000	.33		6000	1380	.23	

[a] All rates of change per $1000
[b] At the upper end of the tax bracket

[17] Its regressive form, $\dfrac{d\,\dfrac{f(Y)}{Y}}{dY} < 0$ for all values of Y, may be ruled out altogether as unacceptable for modern income taxation.

[18] For a discussion of these measures of progressivity see PIGOU, *op. cit.*, pp. 49–50; also R. A. MUSGRAVE AND TUN THIN, "Income Tax Progression, 1929–48," *Journal of Political Economy*, LVI (December, 1948).

[19] PIGOU, *op. cit.*, p. 49.

increases, a much more restrictive condition, indeed, than his own.[20] Table 2 presents a hypothetical income tax which fulfills all four of Pigou's conditions yet gives rise to the inconsistency discussed here. The average rate of this tax increases throughout, as income increases (col. 6), the rate of change of the average rate is positive throughout (col. 7) indicating that the tax is progressive over its whole range, while the rate of change of the marginal rate is alternatingly positive and negative (col. 3) indicating that the tax is mixed progressive-regressive. Similar examples can easily be constructed, because the average rate will always increase (that is, its rate of change will be positive throughout), provided the marginal rate exceeds it at every income level for which the tax liability is greater than zero, regardless of whether the marginal rate rises or falls.

In the light of these considerations, it seems desirable to replace Pigou's second and third tax criterion by the following one:

TAX CRITERION II: THE MARGINAL RATE SHALL BE NON-DECREASING FOR ALL INCREASES IN INCOME

This condition rules out an effective administrative ceiling level of the average rate, such as the 87 per cent ceiling of the United States federal income tax.[21] Such ceiling levels of the average rate, which either arrest or reverse tax progressivity (depending on whether it is measured by the rate of change of the average rate or of the marginal rate) at the upper end of the income scale, have been ruled out by some writers on various grounds, such as inconsistency with principles of equity and "least aggregate sacrifice."[22]

---

[20] *Ibid.* For a more explicit treatment, see *Mathematical Appendix* to Chapter i.

[21] *U.S. Internal Revenue Code; 1954 Code Edition* (Chicago, New York, Washington: Commerce Clearing House, Inc., 1954), Sec. 1(c) states that "the tax shall in no event exceed 87 per cent of the taxable income for the taxable year," whereas the marginal-rate schedule reaches its maximum at 91 per cent. Similarly, a 70 per cent tax ceiling was established for the German income tax in 1953 ("Kleine Steuerreform," June 24, 1953. See HENRY LAUFENBURGER, "Die Einkommensbesteuerung," in *Handbuch der Finanzwissenschaft*, ii (2nd ed.), p. 483).

[22] For example, G. A. D. PREINREICH, "Progressive Taxation and Sacrifice," *American Economic Review*, xxxviii (March, 1948), pp. 109–111.

At this point it is worth noticing that tax criterion II is open to two distinct interpretations, depending on the meaning of the concept "marginal rate." There exist two types of marginal rate which usually, but not necessarily, coincide. First, there is the statutory marginal rate, specified by the tax law, which is applied directly to the increment in taxable income within a given income range. This is the marginal rate which appears in the rate schedules of most tax codes.[23] Thus, if this concept of the marginal rate is used, tax criterion II holds whenever the statutory marginal-rate schedule is one of steadily increasing marginal rates. We shall refer to this (in Section C of this chapter) as the weaker form of criterion II. Its stronger, or more restrictive, form refers to the effective marginal rate, which is the first derivative of the revenue function.[24] It requires that the effective marginal rate be a non-decreasing function of net income (as distinct from taxable income).[25] The two types of marginal rate may differ from each other under certain conditions; for example, when an initial exemption or a vanishing exemption is employed.[26]

We have presented here in some detail the difference between the weaker and the stronger, or more restrictive, form of tax criterion II, because it will be of importance for the analysis in Section C of this chapter.

It is surprising that Pigou's four tax criteria do not provide for preservation of income-rank; that is, PIGOU does not stipulate that the effective marginal rate shall never exceed one hundred per cent. His fourth condition stipulates that the average rate always be less than one hundred per cent, but, of course, this stipulation does not rule out marginal rates in excess of one hundred per cent.[27] Even

---

[23] For example, see *U.S. Internal Revenue Code, 1954 Code Edition*, Sec. 1 (a), (b).

[24] For a mathematical statement of the two types of "marginal rate" and the difference between them, see *Mathematical Appendix* to Chapter I.

[25] It will be noticed that "net income" and "taxable income" are used throughout as technical terms according to the definitions in Section A of this chapter.

[26] This matter will be taken up further in Section C of this chapter.

[27] If the marginal rate reached and maintained a level above 100 per cent,

the "least aggregate sacrifice doctrine" in its purest form, while advocating equalization of income-ranks for the top income ranges, could never justify an actual shifting of income-ranks.[28] Thus, instead of Pigou's fourth tax criterion we shall postulate an income-rank preserving criterion:

TAX CRITERION III: OF ANY TWO AMOUNTS OF INCOME THE ONE THAT IS LARGER PRIOR TO THE DEDUCTION OF THE INCOME TAX LIABILITY SHALL ALSO BE LARGER AFTER THE DEDUCTION

This third tax criterion (together with tax criterion I) will guarantee Pigou's fourth condition. It implies that the effective marginal rate be less than one hundred per cent. It is very unlikely that a country will introduce an explicit marginal rate of one hundred per cent or more, but an income tax with a certain type of exemption may have a small statutory marginal rate while its effective marginal rate exceeds one hundred per cent.[29]

Minor violations of the rank-preserving criterion may not be of great consequence; however, major violations are likely to have a very undesirable effect on incentives to work. Granted that some net disutility is part of the income-earning process and that the possession of additional income gives rise to some net satisfaction or utility,[30] then nobody can be expected to earn more income, if, as

---

the average rate would not be bounded at, or below, 100 per cent. However, we noticed before that Pigou's conditions do not rule out declines in the marginal-rate schedule; thus, they permit marginal rates in excess of 100 per cent, provided they do not persist long enough so as to pull the average rate above 100 per cent.

[28] For an exposition of the "least aggregate sacrifice doctrine" see F. Y. EDGEWORTH, "The Pure Theory of Taxation," in *Papers Relating to Political Economy* (London: Macmillan and Co., Ltd., 1925), II, pp. 63–125; also, PIGOU, *op. cit.*, Pt. II, Chaps. I, IV, V, VI. Both writers stress the fact that even rank-equalization of top incomes would have to be modified because of considerations connected with economic growth and incentives to work (see esp. EDGEWORTH, *op. cit.*, pp. 100–107, and PIGOU, *op. cit.*, Pt. II, Chap. IV, § 7–8 and Chap. V, § 6).

[29] This point will be taken up in Section C of this chapter.

[30] This net disutility of the income-earning process need not imply that work is painful. One has merely to assume that the pleasure of work is outweighed by the opportunity pleasure of leisure (see RICHARD A. MUSGRAVE,

a result of this, he will be left with less disposable income, at least not if the individual is aware of this arrangement.

It is all the more surprising to notice how often tax criterion III has been violated in the past.[31] Even the United States federal income tax contains at least some minor violations of this criterion in the tax table for persons who use the "standard deduction" and have an "adjusted gross income" of less than $5,000. For example, a single person without dependents who had an "adjusted gross income" of $1,999 in 1959 was left with an income after tax of $1,761, whereas an "adjusted gross income" of $2,000 would have left him with only $1,758 after the tax.[32] As long as these violations are small, their disincentive effect is likely to be negligible. Thus, they can be considered the price paid by some taxpayers in order to avail themselves of the convenience of the tax table. Hence, tax criterion III should be interpreted as a general guide rather than an absolutely inviolable principle.[33] Viewed in this manner, it prescribes that no violation of income-rank preservation should be an *inherent part* of the tax structure, or at least, that any such violation should be negligibly small.

In general, tax criterion III will be violated whenever the tax structure is such that either fixed amounts of tax liability or fixed average rates are assigned to the various income ranges,[34] or when initial

---

The Theory of Public Finance (New York, Toronto, London: McGraw-Hill Book Co., Inc., 1959), p. 233).

[31] For example, Kanton Zug, (Switzerland); see PIERRE FOLLIET, *Les Tarifs d'Impôts; Essai de Mathématiques Fiscales* (Lausanne: Librairie Payot, 1947), pp. 95–97; also England, Italy, and Poland; see BRÄUER, *op. cit.*, pp. 83-88, 177, 179. Perhaps the most striking example is that of British income taxation in 1948. In that year, a one-year "special contribution" was levied on the investment income of richer individuals, on top of their income tax and surtax, which resulted in an effective marginal rate of 147.5% (see *The Economist*, April 10, 1948).

[32] See *U.S. Internal Revenue Code; 1954 Code Edition*, Sec. 3.

[33] To a lesser extent, the same holds, of course, with regard to tax criteria I and II.

[34] See FOLLIET, *op. cit.*, pp. 69–88; also BRÄUER, *op. cit.*, pp. 27–40. FOLLIET calls the former "impôt à tarif de quantités"—the latter "impôt à tarif de taux globaux." BRÄUER calls them "Stufenbetragstarif" and "Stufensatz-tarif," respectively.

exemptions or certain types of vanishing exemptions are used.[35]

At this point, it may be useful to return to our graphic presentation in order to determine which types of tax function remain consistent with our three tax criteria. This is done in Plate I where a tax function consistent with Pigou's four tax conditions which is, however, neither convex nor rank-preserving is contrasted with a tax function consistent with our own three tax criteria. The more restrictive nature of our own tax criteria is quite conspicuous. Both sets of criteria limit the income tax functions to that part of the first quadrant of the co-ordinate system which lies below the forty-five degree line through the origin. But Pigou's criteria merely call for a tax function which passes through the origin and is star-shaped with regard to the origin,[36] whereas our own criteria require that the tax function be convex and that none of its tangents have a slope equal to, or exceeding, one.

Finally, a fourth and last restrictive condition deserves to be mentioned here, not as a generally accepted tax criterion for a properly designed income tax function (so far, it has always been violated by past and present income taxes), but rather as a guide for future improvements in income taxation. It deals with the temporal aspects of the accounting period for income taxation and may be formulated in the following way:

TAX CRITERION IV: THE TAX BURDEN OF ANY GIVEN TAXPAYER—INCLUDING IMPUTED INTEREST—SHOULD REMAIN UNCHANGED BY ANY SHIFTS IN THE WAY HIS TOTAL INCOME IS ALLOCATED TO THE VARIOUS INCOME-TAX ACCOUNTING PERIODS (YEARS)[37]

---

[35] See discussion in Section C of this chapter; also BRÄUER, op. cit., pp. 82–90. His "Abzüge gestaffelter Beträge" is such a type of vanishing exemption.

[36] In this connection, the relevant characteristics of the star-shaped function is the following one: The angles of the lines connecting subsequent points on the tax function with the origin must be non-decreasing (this corresponds, of course, to Pigou's third tax condition in its progressive form).

[37] Since we are concerned here with various time paths of the total income stream, total income is not simply the arithmetic sum of all income components accrued, or realized, over the time period under consideration, but rather the total *discounted* value of these components at a specific point of time.

The marginal tax rate is equal to the slope of the tax function
The average tax rate is equal to the slope of the line
which connects the tax function with the origin

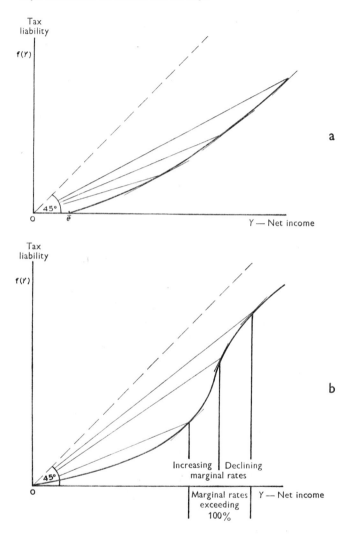

PLATE I. Comparison of a convex rank-preserving income tax function (a) with an income tax function consistent with Pigou's four tax conditions which is neither convex nor rank-preserving (b)

The current violations of this condition under progressive income taxation are obvious. With progressive marginal rates, an individual whose income fluctuates from year to year will pay a heavier tax than an individual having the same average income more evenly distributed from year to year. However, even under proportional taxation without exemptions, violations of criterion IV are likely to occur; for example, a delay in the realization of income for tax purposes is likely to result in interest earnings on that part of the income which otherwise would have been surrendered to the tax authority. Only a comprehensive averaging scheme which imputes interest to both income and tax payments will be entirely consistent with criterion IV.[38] In absence of such a comprehensive scheme, an analysis of income tax exemptions should at least consider the ways in which different treatments of these exemptions may mitigate, or aggravate, the inequities which tend to arise from violations of tax criterion IV.

C. The Exemptions and the Tax Criteria

In the preceding section, three generally accepted tax criteria and a fourth one of a somewhat more utopian-prescriptive nature were presented. At present, it remains to determine to what extent, and under which circumstances, the various types of income tax exemption are consistent with these conditions. Some types of exemption may then be dismissed as unsuited for a properly designed income tax.

Tax criterion I is fulfilled by the very definition of the exemptions. With regard to tax criterion II, we have to distinguish between its weaker and its stronger, or more restrictive, form. In its weaker form, criterion II is not at all affected by the exemption, that is, if successive statutory marginal rates are non-decreasing before the imposition of an exemption, they will also be non-decreasing there-

---

[38] Such a comprehensive averaging scheme was first proposed by Professor VICKREY as early as 1939 (WILLIAM VICKREY, "Averaging of Income for Income Tax Purposes," *Journal of Political Economy*, XLVII (June, 1939), pp. 379–397). It is also incorporated in WILLIAM VICKREY, *Agenda for Progressive Taxation* (New York: The Ronald Press Co., 1947), Chap. 6.

after. However, in its more restrictive form, criterion II may well be affected by the exemption, that is, the effective marginal rate may be changed by the imposition of an exemption. Such a change will almost certainly represent a violation of tax criterion II, if it violates tax criterion III.[39] Therefore, we shall first establish the conditions necessary and sufficient to prevent a violation of criterion III. Then, we shall determine the additional restrictions required to guarantee criterion II in its more restrictive form.

1. INITIAL EXEMPTIONS

Tax criterion III postulates that the income tax be income-rank preserving, that is, that the increment to net income exceed the increment to the tax liability at all income levels. Thus, with regard to the exemption, a necessary and sufficient condition for the fulfillment of criterion III is that the ratio of the increment of taxable income to the increment of net income be smaller than the reciprocal of the statutory marginal rate, that is, that the product of the statutory marginal rate times the rate of change of taxable income be smaller than one.[40]

From Table 1 (p. 7) line 10 and from Fig. 2 (p. 8) we see immediately that only an infinitely small marginal rate could fulfill this condition at the level where net income is equal to the initial exemption $(Y = \bar{e})$, provided that net income were perfectly divisible. However, if income is measured in discrete units, a somewhat larger marginal rate would satisfy condition III. Nevertheless, this rate would be likely to be much too small to be of any practical value. For example, if net income were rounded to the nearest dollar, then for an initial exemption of $600 the statutory marginal rate of the first income bracket would have to be less than 0.17 of one per cent in order that criterion III be not violated. Thus, for all practical purposes tax criterion III rules out the initial exemption. Furthermore, the initial exemption always violates tax criterion II in its more restric-

---

[39] If the imposition of the exemption results in an effective marginal rate exceeding 100% for certain low income levels, successive effective marginal rates cannot be non-decreasing, unless effective marginal rates are to be in excess of 100% for all of the remaining upper part of the income scale.

[40] See *Mathematical Appendix* to Chapter I.

tive form. Therefore, the initial exemption will be dismissed from subsequent chapters of this study.[41]

2. VANISHING EXEMPTIONS

Since exemptions declining by steps have the same kind of jumps as the one of the initial exemption, the same argument applies to them. Comparing Figure 1 with Figure 2, it is apparent that the initial exemption can be viewed as a special case of the exemption declining by steps: a one-step decline.

In case of a linearly declining exemption, tax criterion III will be fulfilled if and only if, over the range of decline of the exemption, the product of the statutory marginal rate times the rate of change of taxable income is less than one. Since, in this case, the rate of change of taxable income is $k + 1$ (where k is the rate of decline of the exemption),[42] this condition can be written $r_i(k + 1) < 1$, where r_i is the statutory marginal rate. The expression $r_i(k + 1)$ stands for the effective marginal rate.[43] Therefore, if the exemption declines linearly (at the rate k) over the first j income brackets, the more restrictive form of tax criterion II will be met if and only if $r_j(k + 1) \leqq r_{j+1}$ (assuming that the weaker form of criterion II is not violated to begin with).[44]

---

[41] As pointed out below, the linearly declining exemption also always violates tax criterion II in its more restrictive form under proportional (but not necessarily under progressive) taxation.

[42] For a linearly declining exemption, over the range of decline, taxable income $(g(Y))$ is given by $g(Y) = (k + 1)(Y - \bar{e})$, where Y stands for net income and $\bar{e}$ for the maximum exemption. Hence $dg/dY = k + 1$ (see also *Mathematical Appendix* to Chapter I).

[43] If R denotes total tax liability; r_i, the statutory marginal rate of the i-th income bracket; then for income which falls within this bracket, the effective marginal rate is given by: $dR/dY = r_i (dg/dY) = r_i(k + 1)$.

[44] It is here assumed that a new tax bracket with a higher *statutory* marginal rate starts at the point where the exemption vanishes. Obviously, otherwise (for example, in the case of a proportional income tax) the more restrictive form of tax criterion II must be violated (see *Mathematical Appendix* to Chapter I). This is due to the fact that the first derivative of the taxable-income function with respect to net income is discontinuous at the point where the exemption vanishes, being $k + 1$ $(k > 0)$ to the left of this point and 1 to its right.

At this point, it becomes rather simple to develop a generalized transformation of a tax with a linearly declining exemption into one with a continuing exemption.[45] The maximum value of the linearly declining exemption ($\bar{e}$) becomes now the continuing exemption and the statutory marginal rates are multiplied by the rate of increase of taxable income ($k + 1$) over the range over which the exemption declines in order to derive the new statutory (and effective) marginal rates. If the tax brackets are stated in terms of taxable income rather than net income (as they usually are), they will also have to be adjusted. Given that g_i is the upper bracket limit of the i-th statutory bracket (expressed in terms of taxable income) for the tax with the linearly declining exemption, then the new bracket limit will be given by $g_i/(k + 1)$ over the range of decline of the exemption and $g_i - \bar{e}$ thereafter.

Table 3 presents an example of such a transformation of a progressive income tax with a linearly declining exemption into an equivalent progressive tax with a continuing exemption. There, a maximum exemption of $\bar{e} = \$500$ and a rate of decline of the linearly declining exemption of $k = .25$ is assumed, so that the exemption declines over a range of $2,000 and vanishes at the net income level $Y = \$2,500$. At a net income level of $2,000, for example, the total tax liability is $375, computed either as a (linearly declining) exemption of $125, plus $62.50 (.10 × 625) on the first $625 of taxable income, plus $125.00 (.20 × 625) on the next $625 of taxable income, plus $187.50 (.30 × 625) on the third $625 of taxable income; or alternately as a (continuing) exemption of $500, plus $62.50 (.125 × 500) on the first $500 of taxable income, plus $125.00 (.250 × 500) on the next $500 of taxable income, plus $187.50 (.375 × 500) on the third $500 of taxable income.

Since any progressive income tax with a linearly declining exemption can be expressed as a progressive tax with a continuing exemption, there will be no need for a separate analysis of the linearly declining exemption under progressive taxation. Hence, this type of exemption is omitted from the analysis in Chapters III and IV. On

---

[45] A systematic derivation is presented in the *Mathematical Appendix* to Chapter I.

TABLE 3. *Transformation of a progressive income tax with a linearly declining exemption into an equivalent progressive income tax with a continuing exemption, assuming a maximum exemption of $\bar{e}$ = $500 and a rate of decline of the linearly declining exemption of k = 0.25*

Tax brackets expressed in terms of net income (Y)	Linearly declining exemption			Continuing exemption ($\dot{e}$ = $500)		
	Upper bracket limit in terms of taxable income ($g(Y)$)	Marginal tax rate	Total tax liability at upper bracket limit	Upper bracket limit in terms of taxable income ($g(Y)$)	Marginal tax rate	Total tax liability at upper bracket limit
	g_i	r_i	R	g_i'	r_i'	$R'=R$
(1)	(2)	(3)	(4)	(5)	(6)	(7)
0– 500	0	0	0	0	0	0
500–1,000	625	.10	62.5	500	.125	62.5
1,000–1,500	1,250	.20	187.5	1,000	.250	187.5
1,500–2,000	1,875	.30	375.0	1,500	.375	375.0
2,000–2,500	2,500[a]	.40	625.0	2,000	.500	625.0
2,500–3,000	3,000	.50	875.0	2,500	.500[b]	875.0
3,000–3,500	3,500	.60	1,175.0	3,000	.600	1,175.0

Notes:

The linearly declining exemption is determined by the following formula: $e(Y) = (k + 1)\bar{e} - kY$, where Y denotes net income; k, the rate of decline of the exemption and $\bar{e}$, the maximum exemption. Hence, in this case, taxable income is given by $g(Y) = (k + 1)(Y - \bar{e})$ for $\bar{e} \le Y < \bar{e} + \bar{e}/k$, and by $g(Y) = Y$ for $Y \ge \bar{e} + \bar{e}/k$. In case of the continuing exemption (which is equal to the maximum exemption $\bar{e}$ = $500), taxable income is always given by $g(Y) = Y - \bar{e}$. Therefore, in this case, the bracket limit expressed in terms of taxable income is equal to the bracket limit expressed in terms of net income minus the maximum (continuing) exemption. Over the range of decline of the linearly declining exemption ($500–2,500), this is also equal to the bracket limit for the latter—expressed in terms of taxable income—divided by $k + 1$ (that is: $g_i' = g_i/(k + 1)$). This downward shift in the tax brackets in terms of taxable income is compensated for by a proportional rise in the statutory marginal-rate schedule (i.e. $r_i' = r_i (k + 1)$ over the range of decline of the exemption).

[a] This is the point $\bar{e} + \bar{e}/k$ at which the exemption vanishes (see *Mathematical Appendix* to Chapter I; also Chapter I, Section A; especially Table 1).

[b] The fact that the marginal rate remains unchanged is the result of the particular example chosen where .50/.40 = 1.25 = $k + 1$. At this point, had the increase in r_i been less than from .40 to .50, the more restrictive form of tax criterion II would have been violated; a sharper increase would have resulted in an increase in r_i'.

the other hand, a proportional tax with a linearly declining exemption cannot be transformed into a proportional tax with a continuing exemption.[46] Therefore, the linearly declining exemption is included in Chapter II which analyzes the exemptions under proportional taxation. This latter analysis may also shed some light on taxes other than the income tax where proportional taxation with an exemption is more commonly applied.

3. CONTINUING EXEMPTIONS

From the preceding discussion it is apparent that the continuing exemption is viewed here as the basic and most important type of income tax exemption. Luckily, this type of exemption raises no serious problems in connection with the three main tax criteria. In this case, the statutory and effective marginal rates co-incide. Hence, if the tax structure is such as to satisfy tax criteria II and III in absence of the exemption, it will continue to do so after the imposition of the exemption.

Before concluding this chapter, some consideration of tax criterion IV is called for. Only a comprehensive averaging scheme could be consistent with this condition which postulates that the tax burden of a given taxpayer—including imputed interest— should remain unchanged by any shifts in the way in which his total income is allocated to the various tax years. However, in absence of such a comprehensive averaging scheme, an "averaging" of income tax exemptions could substantially mitigate some of the inequities which arise from the violations of criterion IV. If the first marginal tax rate is high and exceeds by far any one of the subsequent rate increments, as it often does,[47] then those taxpayers

---

[46] If $\bar{r}$ is the proportional (statutory) tax rate, then over the range of decline of the exemption, the effective marginal rate is $\bar{r}(k + 1) > \bar{r}$ and thereafter it is $\bar{r}$. Hence, our tax transformation will result in two different marginal rates rather than in a single proportional rate. Of course, as mentioned earlier, tax criterion II in its stricter form will be violated.

[47] For example, in case of the U.S. federal income tax, the first marginal rate is 20 per cent while the largest subsequent rate increment is merely five percentage points. Most rate increments are either three or four percentage points (see *U.S. Internal Revenue Code; 1954 Code Edition*, Section 1 (a), (b)).

whose income fluctuates above and below the exemption level are likely to suffer most severely from the violations of criterion IV. A carry-over of the unused part of the exemption would eliminate this inequity without excessive administrative difficulties. In addition, carry-back would increase the countercyclical properties of the income tax while avoiding the awkward question of the starting point of the averaging period which would have to be determined in case of carry-forward. However, carry-back would require actual refunds, while carry-forward would merely result in credits against future income tax liabilities. Hence, from the point of view of fiscal policy carry-back appears preferable, while carry-forward may be preferred for purely administrative reasons.

CHAPTER II

THE EXEMPTIONS UNDER PROPORTIONAL TAXATION

This chapter analyzes the various aspects of the linearly declining and the continuing exemptions under proportional taxation. First, the absolute tax value of the exemption in terms of tax relief as well as its impact on the average tax rate and on tax progressivity will be determined. Then, the effect of changes in the parameters of the tax (viz., the rate at which the exemption declines, the tax rate, and the size of the maximum exemption) will be analyzed.

To-day, most income taxes are progressive in the sense of progression of the marginal tax rates. Nevertheless, a thorough analysis of the "proportional" income tax is well justified, since most analytical concepts and many of the results of the analysis may be directly applied to the more complex "progressive tax." Furthermore, this analysis is useful for a host of widely used proportional taxes other than the income tax. It is for this reason that the linearly declining exemption has been retained in this chapter, in spite of the fact that such an exemption, coupled with a *proportional* tax, always violates tax criterion II in its more restrictive form.[1] (It will be remembered that, in contrast to the progressive tax with a linearly declining exemption which can always be transformed into an equivalent progressive tax with a continuing exemption, no such transformation is possible in case of a "proportional" tax.)[2]

A. The Absolute Tax Value of the Exemption under Proportional Taxation

We define the absolute tax value of the exemption as the amount of money saved by the taxpayer because of the exemption, i.e., the

---

[1] See Chapter I, Section C.

[2] *Ibid.*

amount by which the taxpayer's income tax liability would be increased, if the exemption were abolished. (This is sometimes called the "tax relief" granted by the exemption.)

For all net income levels below the maximum exemption the absolute tax value of the exemption is equal to the product of the tax rate times net income, and reaches its maximum at that level. This statement holds for all types of exemption. At higher net income levels, the absolute tax value of the exemption declines linearly from its maximum value to zero in case of a linearly declining exemption; it remains at its maximum level in case of a continuing exemption.

In general, the absolute tax value of the exemption depends on the values of all three parameters of the tax, that is, the rate at which the exemption declines (k), the tax rate $(\bar{r})$, and the maximum exemption $(\bar{e})$. The smaller the rate at which the exemption declines, ceteris paribus, the larger is the range over which the absolute tax

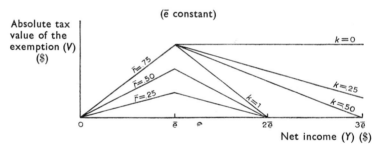

Fig. 4. The effect of changes in the proportional tax rate $(\bar{r})$ and in the rate of decline of the exemption (k) on the absolute tax value (V) of a continuing or linearly declining exemption

Notes:
    $\bar{r}$ denotes the (proportional) tax rate.
    k denotes the rate of decline of the exemption.
    $\bar{e}$ denotes the "maximum exemption," that is, the maximum amount of net income which is tax exempt.

value of the exemption exceeds zero. The higher the tax rate, ceteris paribus, the larger is the rate of change of the absolute tax value of the exemption; and the larger the maximum exemption

ceteris paribus, the larger are the ranges over which the absolute
tax value of the exemption increases and declines and the larger is
its maximum value.[3] A graphical illustration of these relations is
found in Figures 4 and 5.

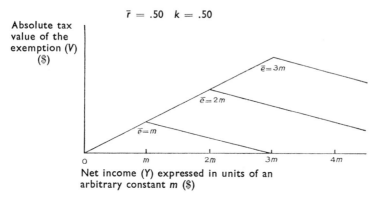

Fig. 5. The effect of changes in the size of the maximum exemption $(\bar{e})$ on
the absolute tax value (V) of a linearly declining exemption

Notes:
$\bar{r}$ denotes the (proportional) tax rate.
k denotes the rate of decline of the exemption.
$\bar{e}$ denotes the "maximum exemption," that is, the maximum amount of
net income which is tax exempt.
Both net income and the maximum exemption are measured in units of
an arbitrary constant m.

B. The Relative Tax Value of the Exemption
under Proportional Taxation

The relative tax value of the exemption (V/Y) is defined as the
absolute tax value of the exemption (V) at a given net income (Y)
divided by this net income. It represents the absolute amount by
which the average tax rate is reduced because of the exemption.
Thus, it measures the absolute impact of the exemption on the
average tax rate. This is illustrated in Table 4, for a continuing
exemption. As shown there, the average tax rate can be computed

---

[3] See also *Mathematical Appendix* to Chapter ii.

by deducting the relative tax value of the exemption from the proportional tax rate (col. 6 = col. 2 — col. 5). From a maximum value equal to the proportional tax rate the relative tax value of

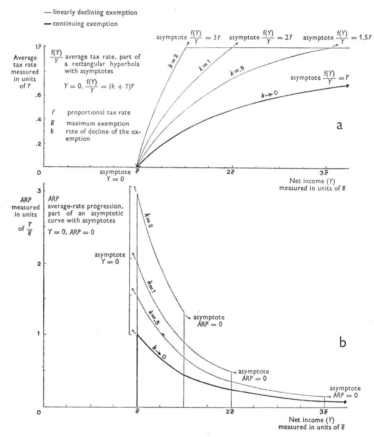

PLATE II. Impact of the rate of decline of the exemption on (a) the average tax rate and (b) the average-rate progression (ARP)

the exemption declines to zero. In mathematical terms the pattern of the relative tax value of the exemption forms part of a declining rectangular hyperbola with the asymptotes $Y = 0$ and $V/Y = -\bar{r}k$.[4]

---

[4] For the continuing exemption ($k = 0$), the second asymptote becomes 0.

As the relative tax value of the exemption declines from $\bar{r}$ to 0, the average tax rate rises from 0 to $\bar{r}$ (see Table 4, cols. 5 and 6). In mathematical terms the pattern of the average rate forms part of a rising rectangular hyperbola with the asymptotes $Y = 0$ and $f(Y)/Y = \bar{r}(k + 1)$.[5] This is shown in diagram (a) of Plate II. Note that net income (Y) is measured on the horizontal axis. If the curves were projected below this axis, that is, beyond the point $Y = \bar{e}$, they

TABLE 4. *Relation between the absolute tax value of the exemption (V), the relative tax value of the exemption (V/Y), and the average tax rate $(f(Y)/Y)$ under proportional taxation with a continuing exemption*

Net income	No exemption		Continuing exemption, $\bar{e} = \$600$		
	Proportional tax rate $\bar{r}$	Average tax rate $f(Y)/Y$	Absolute tax value of the exemption $V = \bar{r}\bar{e}$	Relative tax value of the exemption $V/Y = \bar{r}\bar{e}/Y$	Average tax rate $f(Y)/Y = \bar{r} - (\bar{r}\bar{e}/Y)$ $(6) = (2) - (5)$
(1)	(2)	(3)	(4)	(5)	(6)
400	.20	.20	80	.200	0
600	.20	.20	120	.200	0
1,000	.20	.20	120	.120	.080
2,000	.20	.20	120	.060	.140
5,000	.20	.20	120	.024	.176
10,000	.20	.20	120	.012	.188
100,000	.20	.20	120	.001	.199

would enter the region of negative average rates (which is irrelevant for the present study) and approach, but never intersect, the vertical axis.

C. Income Tax Progression under Proportional Taxation with an Exemption

In the preceding chapter (Section B) we noticed that the progressive nature of the income tax is uniquely established by the

---

[5] For a derivation of all the basic formulae, see *Mathematical Appendix* to Chapter II.

stronger, or more restrictive, form of tax criterion II, regardless of how progressivity is measured. However, the degree of progressivity is not uniquely determined; it depends, rather, on the particular measure used to determine the degree of progressivity. Under certain conditions, different measures may even lead to contradictory results.[6] This limitation (which cannot be avoided) should be kept in mind with regard to our analysis. In our case, the choice of the particular measure is determined by the problem in hand. The "average-rate progression" (henceforth abbreviated "ARP")[7]— which is the rate of change of the average rate per unit increase in net income—is likely to be the most appropriate measure of progressivity in case of an analysis of the impact of the exemption on the tax structure.[8] Hence, whenever we shall refer to a change in the progressivity of the tax, this is to be interpreted as a change in the ARP.

Under proportional taxation, the ARP is zero for incomes below the maximum exemption. At the point where net income equals the maximum exemption, the ARP jumps to its maximum value and declines thereafter. The pattern of decline forms part of an asymptotic curve with the asymptotes $Y = 0$ and ARP $= 0$. For a linearly declining exemption, the ARP is zero beyond the income level at which the exemption vanishes. For the continuing exemption, the ARP declines asymptotically throughout without ever reaching zero. In this way, the exemption transforms the proportional tax into one of steadily declining progressivity.[9] This is illustrated in diagram (b) of Plate II.[10]

---

[6] A certain tax change may increase progressivity as measured by, say, the rate of change of the average rate and may reduce it as measured by the rate of change of the marginal rate.

[7] See R. A. MUSGRAVE AND TUN THIN, "Income Tax Progression, 1929–48," *Journal of Political Economy*, LVI (December, 1948), pp. 499–503.

[8] The reasoning in support of this statement is somewhat elaborate. Instead of inserting at this point a rather lengthy digression, I have decided to present the argument at the end of this chapter in form of a short *Note to Chapter II*.

[9] For a rigorous mathematical treatment, see *Mathematical Appendix* to Chapter II.

[10] In Plates II and III, the ARP is measured in units of $\bar{r}/\bar{e}$. This represents

D. The Impact on the Average Tax Rate and the Average-Rate Progression (ARP) of Changes in the Rate of Decline of the Exemption, the Proportional Tax Rate, and the Size of the Maximum Exemption

As will be seen later, the analysis of the exemption under proportional taxation forms the basis for the analysis of the exemption under progressive taxation. Therefore, changes in the basic parameters of the tax $(k, \bar{r}, \bar{e})$ will be analyzed in detail at present. Much of this analysis can be applied to progressive taxation with very little modification.

1. CHANGES IN THE RATE OF DECLINE OF THE EXEMPTION (k)

In the preceding chapter (Section A, § 4) we noticed that the linearly declining exemption declines over the range $\bar{e} \leq Y \leq \bar{e} + \bar{e}/k$ and that the size of this range $(\bar{e}/k)$ is reduced, whenever the rate of decline of the exemption (k) is increased. More specifically, whenever the rate of decline of the exemption is increased (reduced) by a certain proportion (a), the size of the range over which the exemption declines is reduced (increased) by the reciprocal proportion $(1/a)$.[11] For example, in Table 1, (p. 7) lines 2–3, 4–5, 5–6, and 6–7 represent, each, a doubling of the rate of decline of the exemption and a halving of the range over which the exemption declines.

With regard to the income range over which both the old and the new average tax rate are positive but smaller than the proportional tax rate, the following relationship holds: Whenever the rate of

---

a convenient transformation of scale which greatly facilitates computations. Let net income be measured in units of the maximum exemption, i.e., $Y = m\bar{e}$.

Then, for $\bar{e} \leq Y \leq \bar{e} + \dfrac{\bar{e}}{k}$, $\mathrm{ARP} = \dfrac{\bar{r}(k+1)\bar{e}}{Y^2} = \dfrac{\bar{r}(k+1)}{m^2\bar{e}}$ (see *Mathematical*

Appendix to Chapter II). Expressed in units of $\bar{r}/\bar{e}$, this reduces to $(k+1)/m^2$ units of $\bar{r}/\bar{e}$. For example, for the continuing exemption $(k = 0)$, at the net income level $Y_1 = \bar{e}$, $\mathrm{ARP}_1 = 1\bar{e}/\bar{r}$; at the level $Y_2 = 2\bar{e}$, $\mathrm{ARP}_2 = 0.25\,\bar{r}/\bar{e}$. For $k = 1$, the corresponding values are $\mathrm{ARP}_1 = 2\bar{r}/\bar{e}$ and $\mathrm{ARP}_2 = 0.5\,\bar{r}/\bar{e}$.

[11] In this section, §§ 1–3, a change by a certain proportion is to be interpreted as the expression of the "new" value as a multiple (or fraction) of the "old" value. For example, if k is the original rate of decline of the exemption and k' is the new one, then an increase of k by the proportion a simply means: $k' = ak = k + k(a-1)$, where $a > 1$.

decline of the exemption is increased by a certain proportion (a), both the average tax rate and the ARP schedules are increased by a smaller proportion $(ak + 1)/(k + 1)$.[12] This relationship is illustrated in Plate II. For example, it will be noticed that the doubling of the rate of decline of the exemption from $k = 1$ to $k = 2$ raises the average rate and the ARP schedules by only fifty per cent. Thus, for a net income $Y = 1.25\bar{e}$ the average rate for $k = 1$ is $0.4\bar{r}$, while for $k = 2$ it is $0.6r$. The corresponding values of the ARP are $1.28\bar{r}/\bar{e}$ and $1.92/\bar{r}\bar{e}$.

On the other hand, if the change in the rate of decline of the exemption is viewed as a change in the rate of increase of taxable income $(k + 1)$, the change of $(k + 1)$ by a certain proportion will give rise to precisely the same proportionate change in both the average rate and the ARP schedules. For example, in Plate II, a movement from $k = 1$ to $k = 2$ represents a fifty per cent increase in the rate of change of taxable income (from $(k + 1) = 2$ to $(k + 1) = 3$) and also a fifty per cent increase in both the average rate and the ARP schedules.

2. CHANGES IN THE PROPORTIONAL TAX RATE $(\bar{r})$

The proportional tax rate does not enter into the determination of the range over which the exemption vanishes; therefore, this range is not affected by changes in the proportional tax rate. Thus, with regard to the whole income range, over which the average tax rate is positive, the following relationship holds: Whenever the proportional tax rate is increased (reduced) by a certain proportion, both the average tax rate and the ARP schedules are increased (reduced) by precisely the same proportion.[13]

3. CHANGES IN THE SIZE OF THE MAXIMUM EXEMPTION $(\bar{e})$

An increase in the size of the maximum exemption by a given

---

[12] This proposition as well as the following ones can easily be verified by inspection from the basic formulae for $f(Y)/Y$ and $[d/dY][f(Y)/Y]$ in the *Mathematical Appendix* to Chapter II.

[13] This can be seen in *Plate II*. There, the vertical scales measure the average tax rate and the ARP in units of $\bar{r}$, resp. $\bar{r}/\bar{e}$. Thus, changes in $\bar{r}$ do not affect the diagrams themselves, but represent a change in the vertical scale.

proportion is equivalent to a corresponding increase in the income range over which the average tax rate (and the ARP) is zero. Furthermore, it results in a proportional increase in the range over which the exemption declines. Over this range, the average tax rate is reduced, i.e., the schedule of the average tax rate is shifted downward. This downward shift is constant in neither absolute or relative amount. Rather, the absolute difference between the old and the new average tax rate is a declining function of income, and—since the average tax rate itself is an increasing function of income—the relative (percentage) difference declines even faster with increases in income. Progressivity, as measured by the ARP, is increased by an increase in the size of the exemption. The increase in the absolute amount of the ARP becomes smaller and smaller as income increases, up to the point where the old ARP schedule drops down to zero. However, at the same time the ARP schedule itself is declining with increases in income, and the relative (percentage) increase in the ARP schedule is found to be exactly in proportion to the relative increase in the size of the maximum exemption. This relationship is illustrated in Plate III, where a fifty per cent increase in the size of the maximum exemption (from $\bar{e}$ to $\bar{e}' = 1.5\bar{e}$) increases the ARP schedule by fifty per cent (from ARP to ARP') over the common range of decline. For example, given $k = 1$, for $Y = 1.5\bar{e}$ the respective values of the ARP are ARP $= 0.89\bar{r}/\bar{e}$ and ARP' $= 1.33\bar{r}/\bar{e}$; for $Y = 2\bar{e}$, the corresponding values are ARP $= 0.50\bar{r}/\bar{e}$ and ARP' $= 0.75\bar{r}/\bar{e}$. Given a continuing exemption $(k = 0)$, the respective values of the ARP become ARP $= 0.44\bar{r}/\bar{e}$ and ARP' $= 0.66\bar{r}/\bar{e}$ for $Y = 1.5\bar{e}$, ARP $= 0.25\bar{r}/\bar{e}$ and ARP' $= 0/38\bar{r}/\bar{e}$ for $Y = 2\bar{e}$ (see Plate IIIb).

Under proportional taxation, the new schedule of the average tax rates can easily be derived from the old one for any given change in the size of the maximum exemption. In general, if the new maximum exemption is equal to a-times the old one, the average tax rate which previously applied to a given net income level will now apply to a-times this net income level. For example, if the exemption is increased by fifty per cent, the average tax rate which previously applied to a net income of $1,000 will now apply to a net income of $1,500, etc. (For an illustration see Plate IIIa).

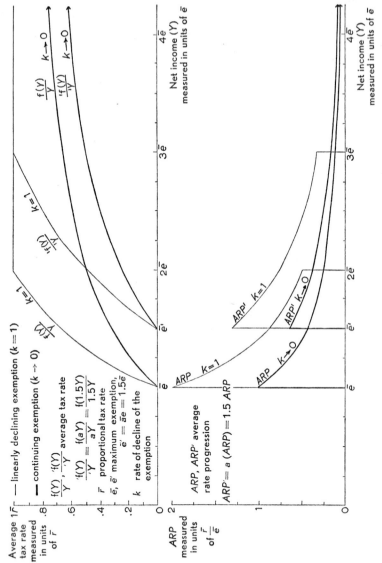

PLATE III. Impact of changes in the size of the exemption on (a) the average tax and (b) the average-rate progression (ARP)

NOTE TO CHAPTER II

On the Choice of the Measure of Tax Progressivity

In Section C of Chapter II, it has been pointed out that the degree of tax progressivity of a given tax varies with the measure of progressivity used. There, the average-rate progression (ARP), that is, the rate of change of the average tax rate, was chosen as a particularly appropriate measure of tax progressivity for this study. The rationale for this choice is not mere ease of computation.

The choice of the measure of progressivity should be determined by the problem in hand. If we want to investigate the degree of progressivity of the marginal rate structure (that is, the degree of progression which exists among successive marginal rates), then marginal-rate progression (MRP), that is, the rate of change of the marginal tax rate, seems an appropriate indicator. If, on the other hand, our interest concentrates largely on the distribution of the average tax burden at different income levels, then the average-rate structure and the rate of change of the average rate (ARP) seem more revealing measures. An analysis of income tax exemptions, by its very nature, is likely to focus on the average tax burden, since changes in the size of a continuing exemption do not modify the marginal rate structure (and hence the MRP) proper, but simply represent a downward shift of net income in relation to this given marginal rate structure.[14] This fact is illustrated in Figure 6 below. As shown there, the imposition of a continuing exemption of $600 simply shifts the zero point of the X-axis by $600 to the left without affecting the marginal-rate structure. Thus, the analysis of the impact of the continuing exemption on the MRP is exhausted by the statement that the exemption pulls certain taxpayers into a lower income bracket. As a matter of fact, Section D of Chapter IV which deals with the incentive effects of changes in the size of the continuing exemption and of tax-rate changes explores this particular result. There, the rate of change of the "net marginal rate of

---

[14] However, in case of a vanishing exemption, a change in the effective marginal rate structure does occur. (See *Chapter I*, Section C, and *Mathematical Appendix* to Chapter I).

remuneration" is found to be a more useful tool of analysis than the MRP.

We can summarize our argument as follows. Our analysis of the income tax exemption focuses mainly on its impact on the distribution of the tax burden. This impact is best indicated by the average rate schedule and its modification by the exemption. The ARP, in this instance, serves as an important supplementary measure, being the first derivative of the average rate with regard to net income.[15] When we deal with problems of incentive effects, the "net marginal rate of remuneration," a marginal measure derived from the marginal tax rate,[16] becomes a major tool of our analysis.

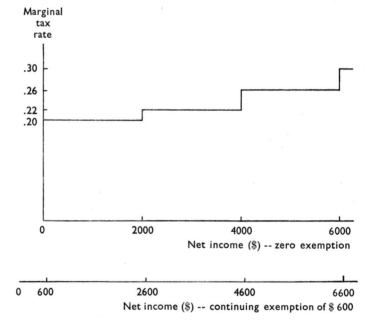

Fig. 6. The effect of changes in the size of a continuing exemption on the marginal-rate structure—an illustration*

* Based on the U.S. federal income tax for single persons with no dependents.

---

[15] This discussion is phrased in terms of "ARP versus MRP." While the ARP and the MRP are the most popular measures of tax progressivity (e.g.,

see PIGOU, *op. cit.*, pp. 50–51), they suffer both from serious deficiencies which I have analyzed and criticized elsewhere ("The Income Elasticity of the Rate of Retained Income as a Measure of Tax Progressivity," an unpublished article). There, I have also suggested what I consider a preferable measure of tax progressivity. However, in a study of this nature, the use of a familiar measure of progressivity seems advisable. Furthermore, the analysis of the ARP should be viewed as a supplement to the analysis of the average tax rate rather than an abstract measure of a somewhat evasive "tax progressivity proper."

[16] The "net marginal rate of remuneration" is equal to the marginal wage rate times one minus the marginal tax rate (see *Chapter IV*, Section D, also *Mathematical Appendix* to Chapter IV).

CHAPTER III

THE CONTINUING EXEMPTION UNDER
PROGRESSIVE TAXATION

The analysis of the exemption under progressive taxation is based on the preceding analysis, but it is much more complex. Later we shall see that the reason for this complexity is found in the fact that the progressive tax structure is equivalent to a series of proportional taxes—each having its own tax rate and exemption—which are applied to the different income ranges.[1]

In this and the following chapter (both of which deal with progressive income taxation), we can eliminate the linearly declining exemption altogether from our discussion, since any progressive tax with a linearly declining exemption can be transformed into an equivalent progressive tax with a continuing exemption through adjustments in the tax rates and brackets.[2] Hence, the continuing exemption will be our sole concern.

In this chapter, we shall follow the same logical order that was established in Chapter II with regard to proportional taxation. First, the absolute and relative tax value of the exemption will be determined. Then, the impact of the exemption on tax progressivity, as measured by the average-rate progression (ARP), will be analyzed. Thereafter, changes in the basic parameters of the tax will be considered. Subsequently, in Chapter IV, changes in tax revenue resulting from a change in the size of the continuing exemption will be compared with those resulting from manipulations of the marginal rate scale.

---

[1] See Section D of this chapter. We use the terms "progressive taxation" and "progressive tax" throughout in reference to a tax constructed of a number of tax brackets to which different marginal rates are applied.

[2] See Chapter I, Section C; also *Mathematical Appendix* to Chapter I.

A. The Absolute Tax Value of the Continuing Exemption under Progressive Taxation

In our analysis we have to differentiate between two cases:

Case I: Where the exemption cuts across the taxable-income bracket; that is, the range over which the exemption shifts the net-income brackets so that they no longer co-incide with the taxable-income brackets.[3] For the present analysis we shall assume that the exemption does not cut across more than one taxable-income bracket at a time. Later, using a somewhat different approach, we shall be able to drop this limitation and to generalize our results.[4]

Case II: Where the exemption is contained in a single taxable-income bracket.

CASE I: *The Exemption Cuts Across the Taxable-Income Bracket*

Where the exemption cuts across the taxable-income bracket, the absolute tax value of the exemption will increase at a rate equal to the difference between the two adjacent marginal tax rates $(r_{n+1} - r_n)$ per unit increase in net income. Thus the bigger the jump in the marginal tax rate, the larger the rate of increase of the absolute tax value of the exemption where it cuts across the net income bracket.[5]

CASE II: *The Exemption Contained in a Single Taxable-Income Bracket*

Where the exemption is contained within a single taxable-income

---

[3] Statutory income brackets are usually defined in terms of taxable income, $g = Y - \bar{e}$, that is, the statutory marginal rates are usually expressed as a function of taxable rather than net income: $r(g)$. The taxable-income brackets are given by the intervals $(0, g_1)$, (g_1, g_2), . . .; where g_1, g_2, . . ., are the points at which $r(g)$ changes value (from r_1 to r_2 to r_3 . . .). The net-income brackets, (Y_i, Y_{i+1}), are simply a translation to the right by the continuing exemption $(\bar{e})$ of the corresponding taxable-income brackets: $(Y_i, Y_{i+1}) = (g_i + \bar{e}, g_{i+1} + \bar{e})$.

The exemption will cut across the taxable-income bracket if $\bar{e} > Y_n - Y$, where Y_n denotes the lowest net-income bracket limit (after imposing the exemption) which exceeds the income level Y. (A more systematic discussion of all this may be found in the *Mathematical Appendix* to Chapter III.)

[4] See Sections D and E of this chapter.

[5] For a more rigorous treatment see *Mathematical Appendix* to Chapter III.

bracket, the absolute tax value of the exemption (V) is a constant equal to the product of the effective marginal rate times the exemption $(V_n = r_n \bar{e})$.[6] Since the marginal tax rate increases from bracket to bracket,[7] this constant also increases from bracket to bracket.

It will be noted that every taxable-income bracket contains, at its lower end, a section where the exemption will cut across it. For the remainder of the bracket, the entire exemption is contained with it. Therefore, the absolute tax value of the exemption alternately increases linearly (at the rate of $r_{n+1} - r_n$) to a relative maximum $(r_{n+1}\bar{e})$ and then remains constant at this maximum, as net income increases within each bracket. This is illustrated in Plate IV which gives the absolute tax value of the exemption for the 1959 United States federal income tax for single persons with no dependents having a net income of $100–$100,000.[8]

B. The Relative Tax Value of the Continuing Exemption under Progressive Taxation

The relative tax value of the exemption is equal to the absolute tax value of the exemption divided by net income. Therefore, the partition of each net income bracket into "Case I" and "Case II" applies in this instance just as in the preceding section.

CASE I: *The Exemption Cuts Across the Taxable-Income Bracket*

As net income moves across a taxable-income bracket limit, and as it moves higher until the exemption is entirely contained in the new bracket, the relative tax value of the exemption either (a)

---

[6] We have shown earlier (*Mathematical Appendix* to Chapter I) that the effective marginal rate and the statutory marginal rate co-incide in case of a continuing exemption.

[7] Tax criterion II. In case of a continuing exemption, the weaker and stronger forms of this criterion co-incide, thus $V_n = r_n\bar{e} < V_{n+1} = r_{n+1}\bar{e}$.

[8] *In Plate IV*, the increase in the absolute tax value of the continuing exemption is curvilinear rather than linear, because of the semi-logarithmic graph paper used. For a presentation on arithmetic graph paper see *Plate XII*.

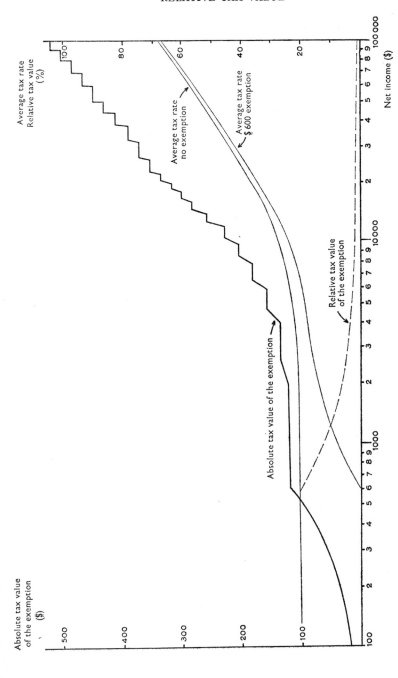

PLATE IV. Absolute and relative tax value of the exemption, average tax rate in absence of the exemption, and effective average tax rate, for single persons with no dependents, according to the 1959 United States federal income tax

declines at a slower rate than it did before net income crossed the bracket limit (i.e., when the entire exemption was contained within the lower taxable-income bracket), or (b) remains constant, or (c) actually increases.

The following condition determines the behavior of the relative tax value of the exemption over any given section, where the exemption cuts across a taxable-income bracket, as described immediately above: The relative tax value of the exemption increases, remains constant, or declines, as net income increases across the bracket limit, depending on whether the exemption falls short of, is equal to, or exceeds, the product of the relative difference between the two adjacent marginal rates times income at the bracket limit where the exemption cuts across the taxable-income bracket.[9]

The following example will demonstrate this condition. The marginal rates of the 1959 United States federal income tax for single persons with no dependents are 20 per cent for the first $2,000, 22 per cent for the next $2,000, and 26 per cent for the third $2,000. Given an exemption of $600, we find that $600 > [(.22—.20)/.20] $2,000 = $200, hence, the relative tax value of the exemption declines over the net income range $2,000–$2,600, that is as long as net income cuts across the $2,000 bracket limit ($2,001, $2,002, etc.) until the exemption is completely contained in the next taxable-income bracket ($2,00–$4,000) at $2,600. However, $600 < [(.26—.22)/.22] $4,000 = $727, hence, the relative tax value of the exemption increases over the net income range $4,000–$4,600. This can be seen from Table 5, column (5). Lines 3–4 show a decline in the relative tax value of the exemption of .003637 for the increase in net income from $2,000 to $2,200, while lines 7–8 show an increase in the relative tax value of the exemption of .000333 for the increase in net income from $4,000 to $4,200.

From the above condition it is obvious that the relative tax value of the exemption is more and more likely to increase, as net income

---

[9] That is, $d(V/Y)/dY \gtrless 0$, depending on whether $[(r_{n+1}-r_n)/r_n]g_n \gtrless \bar{e}$. For a derivation of this condition and for a more explicit treatment, see *Mathematical Appendix* to Chapter III.

increases, over the section where the exemption cuts across a given taxable-income bracket, the higher this income bracket. For example, in case of the 1959 United States federal income tax for single persons with no dependents, the relative tax value of the exemption increases over all sections where the exemption cuts across the taxable-income bracket, except for the transition from the first to the second bracket (see Table 5, column (5)).[10]

TABLE 5. *Absolute and relative tax value of the exemption and impact of the exemption on the average tax rate and on progressivity; 1959 United States federal income tax for single persons with no dependents*

Net income Y ($000)	Top marginal rate v_n	Absolute tax value of the exemption V	Average rate in absence of the exemption $f(Y + \bar{e})/Y$	Relative tax value of the exemption V/Y	Effective average rate $f(Y)/Y$	Percentage impact of the exemption on progressivity $(6) = (4) - (5)$	No. of top income bracket
(1)	(2)	(3)	(4)	(5)	(6)	(7)	(8)
1.0	.20	120	.200000	.120000	.080000		1
1.2	.20	120	.200000	.100000	.100000	100.0	
2.0	.20	120	.200000	.060000	.140000		1–2
2.2	.22	124	.201818	.056363	.145454	66.7	
3.0	.22	132	.206666	.044000	.162666		2
3.2	.22	132	.207500	.041250	.166250	76.7	
4.0	.22	132	.210000	.033000	.177000		2–3
4.2	.26	140	.212381	.033333	.179047	—16.3	
5.0	.26	156	.220000	.031200	.188800		3
5.2	.26	156	.221538	.030000	.191538	43.8	

[10] In Table 5, the ranges where the exemption cuts across the taxable-income bracket are indicated by the two relevant bracket numbers in column (8), such as 1–2, 2–3, etc. A single bracket number (1, 2, etc.) in column (8) indicates that net income falls within the same taxable-income and net-income bracket at the given income level.

TABLE 5. *(continued)*

Net income Y ($000)	Top marginal rate r_n	Absolute tax value of the exemption V	Average rate in absence of the exemption $f(Y + \bar{e})/Y$	Relative tax value of the exemption V/Y	Effective average rate $f(Y)/Y$ $(6) = (4) - (5)$	Percentage impact of the exemption on progressivity	No. of top income bracket
(1)	(2)	(3)	(4)	(5)	(6)	(7)	(8)
6.0	.26	156	.226666	.026000	.200666		3–4
6.2	.30	164	.229032	.026451	.202580	—23.6	
7.0	.30	180	.237142	.025714	.211428		4
7.2	.30	180	.238888	.025000	.213888	29.0	
8.0	.30	180	.245000	.022500	.222500		4–5
8.2	.34	188	.247317	.022926	.224390	—22.5	
9.0	.34	204	.255555	.022666	.232888		5
9.2	.34	204	.257391	.022173	.235217	21.2	
10.0	.34	204	.264000	.020400	.243600		5–6
10.2	.38	212	.266274	.020784	.245490	—20.3	
11.0	.38	228	.274545	.020727	.253818		6
11.2	.38	228	.276428	.020357	.256071	16.4	
12.0	.38	228	.283333	.019000	.264333		6–7
12.2	.43	238	.285737	.019508	.266229	—26.8	
13.0	.43	258	.294615	.019846	.274769		7
13.2	.43	258	.296666	.019545	.277121	12.8	
14.0	.43	258	.304285	.018428	.285857		7–8
14.2	.47	266	.306619	.018732	.287887	—14.9	
15.0	.47	282	.315333	.018800	.296533		8
15.2	.47	282	.317368	.018552	.298815	10.8	
16.0	.47	282	.325000	.017625	.307375		8–9
16.2	.50	288	.327160	.017777	.309382	—7.6	
17.0	.50	300	.335294	.017647	.317647		9
17.2	.50	300	.337209	.017441	.319767	9.7	
18.0	.50	300	.344444	.016666	.327777		9–10
18.2	.53	306	.346483	.016813	.329670	—7.7	

TABLE 5. *(continued)*

Net income Y ($000)	Top marginal rate v_n	Absolute tax value of the exemption V	Average rate in absence of the exemption $f(Y+\bar{e})/Y$	Relative tax value of the exemption V/Y	Effective average rate $f(Y)/Y$ (6) = (4) — (5)	Percentage impact of the exemption on progressivity	No. of top income bracket
(1)	(2)	(3)	(4)	(5)	(6)	(7)	(8)
19.0	.53	318	.354210	.016736	.337473		10
19.2	.53	318	.356041	.016562	.339479	8.7	
20.0	.53	318	.363000	.015900	.347100		10–11
20.2	.56	324	.364950	.016039	.348910	—7.7	
21.0	.56	336	.372380	.016000	.356380		11
21.2	.56	336	.374150	.015849	.358301	7.8	
22.0	.56	336	.380909	.015272	.365636		11–12
22.2	.59	342	.382792	.015405	.367387	—7.5	
24.0	.59	354	.398333	.014750	.383583		12
24.2	.59	354	.399917	.014628	.385289	7.1	
26.0	.59	354	.413076	.013615	.399461		12–13
26.2	.62	360	.414656	.013740	.400915	—8.6	
29.0	.62	372	.434482	.012827	.421655		13
29.2	.62	372	.435753	.012739	.423013	6.4	
32.0	.62	372	.451875	.011625	.440250		13–14
32.2	.65	378	.453105	.011739	.441366	—10.2	
35.0	.65	390	.468857	.011142	.457714		14
35.2	.65	390	.469886	.011079	.458806	5.8	
38.0	.65	390	.483157	.010263	.472894		14–15
38.2	.69	396	.484240	.010366	.473874	—10.5	
41.0	.69	414	.498292	.010097	.488195		15
41.2	.69	414	.499223	.010048	.489174	5.0	
44.0	.69	414	.511363	.009409	.501954		15–16
44.2	.72	420	.512262	.009502	.502760	—11.6	
47.0	.72	432	.524680	.009191	.515489		16
47.2	.72	432	.525508	.009152	.516355	4.5	

TABLE 5.   (*continued*)

Net income Y ($000)	Top marginal rate r_n	Absolute tax value of the exemption V	Average rate in absence of the exemption $f(Y + \bar{e})/Y$	Relative tax value of the exemption V/Y	Effective average rate $f(Y)/Y$ (6) = (4) — (5)	Percentage impact of the exemption on progressivity	No. of top income bracket
(1)	(2)	(3)	(4)	(5)	(6)	(7)	(8)
50.0	.72	432	.536400	.008640	.527760		16–17
50.2	.75	438	.537250	.008725	.528525	—11.1	
55.0	.75	450	.555818	.008181	.547636		17
55.2	.75	450	.556521	.008152	.548369	4.0	
60.0	.75	450	.572000	.007500	.564500		17–18
60.2	.78	456	.572691	.007574	.565116	—12.1	
65.0	.78	468	.588000	.007200	.580800		18
65.2	.78	468	.588588	.007177	.581411	3.6	
70.0	.78	468	.601714	.006685	.595028		18–19
70.2	.81	474	.602307	.006752	.595555	—12.6	
75.0	.81	486	.615600	.006480	.609120		19
75.2	.81	486	.616117	.006462	.609654	3.2	
80.0	.81	486	.627750	.006075	.621675		19–20
80.2	.84	492	.628279	.006134	.622144	—12.7	
85.0	.84	504	.640235	.005929	.634305		20
85.2	.84	504	.640704	.005915	.634788	2.9	
90.0	.84	504	.651333	.005600	.645733		20–21
90.2	.87	510	.651818	.005654	.646164	—12.6	
95.0	.87	522	.662842	.005494	.657347		21
95.2	.87	522	.663277	.005483	.657794	2.6	
100.0	.87	522	.673200	.005220	.667980		21–22
100.2	.89	526	.673632	.005249	.668383	—7.3	
125.0	.89	534	.716560	.004272	.712288		22
125.2	.89	534	.716837	.004265	.712571	2.4	
150.0	.89	534	.745466	.003560	.741906		22–23
150.2	.90	536	.745672	.003568	.742103	—4.3	

TABLE 5.   *(continued)*

Net income Y ($000)	Top marginal rate r_n	Absolute tax value of the exemption V	Average rate in absence of the exemption $f(Y+e)/Y$	Relative tax value of the exemption V/Y	Effective average rate $f(Y)/Y$ $(6) = (4) - (5)$	Percentage impact of the exemption on progressivity	No. of top income bracket
(1)	(2)	(3)	(4)	(5)	(6)	(7)	(8)
175.0	.90	540	.767542	.003085	.764457		23
175.2	.90	540	.767694	.003082	.764611	2.3	
200.0	.90	540	.784100	.002700	.781400		23–24
200.2	.91	542	.784225	.002707	.781518	—6.1	
300.0	.91	546	.826066	.001820	.824246		24
300.2	.91	546	.826122	.001818	.824303	2.1	

Notes:

(1) Net income — Y; taken at midpoint and endpoint of each taxable-income bracket for an interval of $200.

(2) Top marginal rate — r_n; highest marginal rate applied to that net income level.

(3) Absolute tax value of the exemption — V; for single bracket numbers (see (8)) $V = r_n \bar{e}$, for double bracket numbers $V = Y_n r_n + (\bar{e} - Y_n) r_{n+1} + (r_{n+1} - r_n) Y$ (see *Mathematical Appendix* to Chapter III).

(4) Average rate in absence of exemptions —$f(Y + \bar{e})/(Y = f(Y) + V/Y$.

(7) Percentage impact of the exemption on progressivity $= [-(\Delta V/\Delta Y)/(\Delta f(Y)/Y)] 100$.

(8) Number of top income bracket — gives the bracket number. If single number, the exemption does not cut across the bracket limit, if double number, it cuts across.

CASE II: *The Exemption Contained in a Single Taxable-Income Bracket*

Within each taxable-income bracket, where the exemption does not cut across the income bracket limit, the relative tax value of the exemption declines, as net income increases. The pattern of this decline forms part of a rectangular hyperbola with the asymptotes

$Y = 0$ and $V/Y = 0.$[11] This case is analogous to the relative tax value of the exemption under proportional taxation with the proportional tax rate equal to the marginal tax rate of the given section.

C. Income Tax Progression under Progressive Taxation with a Continuing Exemption

The impact of the exemption on the average tax rate and the average-rate progression (ARP) is defined as the difference between the rate which would prevail in absence of the exemption and the actual effective rate. The average tax rate which would prevail in absence of the exemption exceeds the effective average tax rate by the relative tax value of the exemption. Thus, the analysis of the preceding section determines the impact of the exemption on the average tax rate.

Within each taxable-income bracket, over the range where the exemption does not cut across the bracket limit, the average tax rate is reduced—and progressivity, as measured by the ARP, is increased—by smaller and smaller amounts, per unit increase in net income, as income increases, though staying within the bracket in question. This can be seen from Table 5, giving the values of the average tax rate in absence of an exemption, $f(Y + \bar{e})/Y$, the relative tax value of the exemption (V/Y), and the effective average tax rate $[f(Y)/Y = f(Y + \bar{e})/Y — (V/Y)]$ for the 1959 United States federal income tax for single persons with no dependents. For example, at net income of $9,000, the exemption reduces the average tax rate from $f(Y + \bar{e})/Y = .255555$ (col. 4) to $f(Y)/Y = .232888$ (col. 6), that is, by $V/Y = .022666$ (col. 5). At net income of $9,200, the corresponding values are $f(Y + \bar{e})/Y = .257391$ (col. 4), $f(Y)/Y = .235217$ (col. 6), and $V/Y = .022173$, that is, the impact of the exemption on the average rate is reduced. Over the net income range $9,000–$9,200 as a whole, the exemption increases tax progressivity by 21.2 per cent of the effective ARP (col. 7).

Over each section where the exemption cuts across the taxable-income bracket, the average tax rate is likely to be reduced, from

---

[11] Over the range under discussion, the relative tax value of the exemption is given by $V/Y = r_n \bar{e}/Y$.

what it would have been without the exemption, by larger and larger amounts, per unit increase in net income, as income increases over this section, and thus the ARP is likely to be reduced by the exemption. Again, this can be seen from Table 5. For example, at net income of $10,000, the exemption reduces the average rate from $f(Y + \bar{e})/Y = .264000$ (col. 4) to $f(Y)/Y = .243600$ (col. 6), that is, by $V/Y = .020400$ (col. 5). At net income of $10,200, the corresponding values are $f(Y + \bar{e})/Y = .266274$ (col. 4), $f(Y)/Y = .245490$ (col. 6), and $V/Y = .020784$ (col. 5), that is, the impact of the exemption on the average rate is increased. Over the net income range $10,000–$10,200 as a whole, the exemption reduces tax progressivity by 20.3 per cent of the effective ARP (col. 7).

Whenever the exemption cuts across a taxable-income bracket limit its impact on the tax rate is equivalent to a shift in the income bracket limit by the amount of the exemption which delays the effective application of the new marginal rate. However, this should not detract from the interesting fact that thereby progressivity is likely to be reduced over this particular income range. For example, in case of the 1959 United States federal income tax for single persons with no dependents with net income up to $22,000, the exemption of $600 reduces progressivity (as measured by the ARP) over about 37 per cent of this range, because the brackets have a width of $2,000.[12]

Before we attempt to analyze changes in the exemption and in the tax rates, it is worth-while to develop a somewhat different approach that will prove to be simpler and more manageable with regard to these problems. This new approach consists of a transformation of the progressive tax into a series of proportional taxes. This transformation permits us to draw more extensively on our analysis of the exemption under proportional taxation and to utilize certain graphic presentations which are extremely helpful.

---

[12] That is, except for the first income bracket, the exemption reduces progressivity over the first $600 of each subsequent net-income bracket (i.e., $4,000–$4,600, $6,000–$6,600, etc.) where it cuts across the taxable-income bracket limit. Since the net income of $22,000 embraces 11 income brackets, the exemption reduces progressivity by 10 times $600, that is, by $6,000 which is about 37 per cent of the total range of $22,000.

D. Transformation of a Progressive Tax into a Series of Proportional Taxes with Exemption

The analysis of the exemption under proportional taxation proved to be relatively simple. Under progressive taxation, it becomes more complex, because each income level which exceeds the first income bracket is partitioned into bracket-sections by a series of income brackets each of which has a different marginal rate. Instead of partitioning each income level into bracket sections, we can partition the whole income range from zero to infinity into "income classes" depending on the top bracket reached by the given income level. For each "income class," a proportional tax with a "bracket-exemption" can be found which has the marginal (bracket-) rate as its proportional tax rate and which yields exactly the same tax liabilities as the progressive tax.[13] In this case, determining the top bracket reached by a certain income is equivalent to assigning a particular proportional tax with (bracket-) exemption to this income.[14]

Table 6 may help to clarify this equivalence. It shows the bracket-exemptions for the 1959 United States federal income tax for single persons with no dependents. The marginal rate (col. 5)—which becomes now the proportional tax rate—and the bracket-exemption (col. 7) provide us with the complete transformation. For example, under progressive taxation, the net income of $7,000 is partitioned into its bracket sections of $0–2,000, $2,000–4,000, $4,000–6,000 and

---

[13] Henceforth, the term "bracket-exemption" will be used to designate the exemption which is applied to a proportional tax that represents a part of the transformation here described. There exists a separate bracket-exemption for each bracket, the first one being the statutory exemption. The *Mathematical Appendix* to Chapter III, contains the derivation of two mathematical formulae for the computation of the bracket-exemption. For actual computations, see *Table 6*.

[14] A different type of tax transformation is used by WILLIAM VICKREY. (See WILLIAM VICKREY, "Some Limits to the Income Elasticity of Income Tax Yields," *Review of Economics and Statistics*, XXXI (May, 1949), pp. 140–144). Instead of assigning each income level to one single proportional tax with an exemption, he applies a basic proportional tax and several proportional "surtaxes," each with a particular exemption.

TABLE 6. *Bracket-exemptions for the 1959 United States federal income tax for single persons with no dependents*

No. of income bracket	Taxable-income bracket ($000)	Net-income bracket ($000)	Net income at lower net-income bracket-limit (Y_{n-1})	Marginal (bracket-) rate r_n	Tax liability at lower bracket-limit ($\$$) $f(Y_{n-1})$	Bracket-exemption ($\$$) $\left(e_n = Y_{n-1} - f(Y_{n-1})/r_n\right)$
(1)	(2)	(3)	(4)	(5)	(6)	(7)
1	0—2	0.6—2.6	0.6	.20	0	600
2	2—4	2.6—4.6	2.6	.22	400	782
3	4—6	4.6—6.6	4.6	.26	840	1,369
4	6—8	6.6—8.6	6.6	.30	1,360	2,067
5	8—10	8.6—10.6	8.6	.34	1,960	2,834
6	10—12	10.6—12.6	10.6	.38	2,640	3,653
7	12—14	12.6—14.6	12.6	.43	3,400	4,693
8	14—16	14.6—16.6	14.6	.47	4,260	5,536
9	16—18	16.6—18.6	16.6	.50	5,200	6,200
10	18—20	18.6—20.6	18.6	.53	6,200	6,902
11	20—22	20.6—22.6	20.6	.56	7,260	7,636
12	22—26	22.6—26.6	22.6	.59	8,380	8,397
13	26—32	26.6—32.6	26.6	.62	10,740	9,277
14	32—38	32.6—38.6	32.6	.65	14,460	10,354
15	38—44	38.6—44.6	38.6	.69	18,360	11,991
16	44—50	44.6—50.6	44.6	.72	22,500	13,350
17	50—60	50.6—60.6	50.6	.75	26,820	14,840
18	60—70	60.6—70.6	60.6	.78	34,320	16,600
19	70—80	70.6—80.6	70.6	.81	42,120	18,600
20	80—90	80.6—90.6	80.6	.84	50,220	20,814
21	90—100	90.6—100.6	90.6	.87	58,620	23,221
22	100—150	100.6—150.6	100.6	.89	67,320	24,960
23	150—200	150.6—200.6	150.6	.90	111,820	26,356
24	200 +	200.6 +	200.6	.91	156,820	28,270

Notes:

(7) Bracket-exemption—the formula used for the computation of the bracket-exemption is $e_n = Y_{n-1} - f(Y_{n-1})/r_n$, that is, column (4) minus (column (6) divided by column (5)). For the derivation of this formula, see *Mathematical Appendix* to Chapter III. As shown there, the *upper* net-income bracket-limit (i.e. the one which just exceeds net income (Y)) and its tax liability ($f(Y_n)$) could have been used to determine e_n (that is: $e_n = Y_n - f(Y_n)/r_n$).

$6,000–6,400 (allowing for a continuing exemption of $600) to which the corresponding marginal rates of 20%, 22%, 26%, and 30% are applied, yielding a total tax liability of $1,480. On the other hand, the net income of $7,000 may be thought of as a member of the fourth income class of $6,600–8,600 (line 4, col. 3) to which a proportional tax of 30% (line 4, col. 5) and a (bracket-) exemption of $2,067 (line 4, col. 7) are assigned. Again, the tax liability is $1,480.

A graphical determination of the bracket-exemptions is presented in Plates v and vii. There, the tax liability is measured along the Y-axis, net income along the X-axis. The heavy-shaded series of connected line segments represents the functional relationship between net income and the tax liability. There exists one such line segment for each net-income bracket, its slope being equal to the marginal rate of that bracket. Since successive marginal rates increase, the line segments get steeper, as income increases. Project any given line segment onto the X-axis (lighter-shaded lines), and the intersection of the projection with the X-axis is the bracket-exemption for the net income range covered by this line segment. For example, the ninth income class, represented by the ix-th line segment, covers the net income range of $16,000–18,000 in absence of a statutory exemption (Plate v) and of $16,600–18,600 in case of a continuing exemption of $600 (Plate vii). The slope of the ix-th line segment is one half, or equal to the marginal rate of 50%. The projection of this line segment (second lighter-shaded line from the right) intersects the X-axis at $5,600 in absence of a statutory exemption (Plate v), or at $6,200 in case of a continuing exemption of $600 (Plate vii), which is equal to the bracket-exemption for the ninth income class.[15]

Effects on the average tax rate and on the average-rate progression (ARP) of changes in the size of the continuing exemption and in the rate structure will be analyzed in Section E of this chapter. However, the general technique of this analysis will be exposed now.

The preceding transformation enables us to apply our analysis of

---

[15] A similar approach, in mathematical terms, may be found in the *Mathematical Appendix* to this chapter.

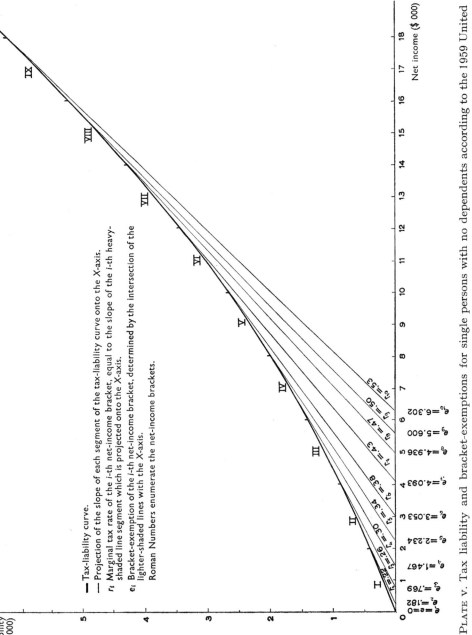

PLATE v. Tax liability and bracket-exemptions for single persons with no dependents according to the 1959 United States federal income tax, in absence of a statutory exemption

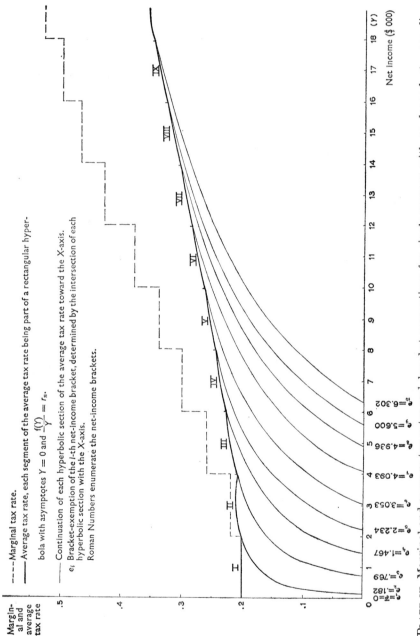

PLATE VI. Marginal and average tax rates and bracket-exemptions for single persons with no dependents according to the 1959 United States federal income tax, in absence of a statutory exemption

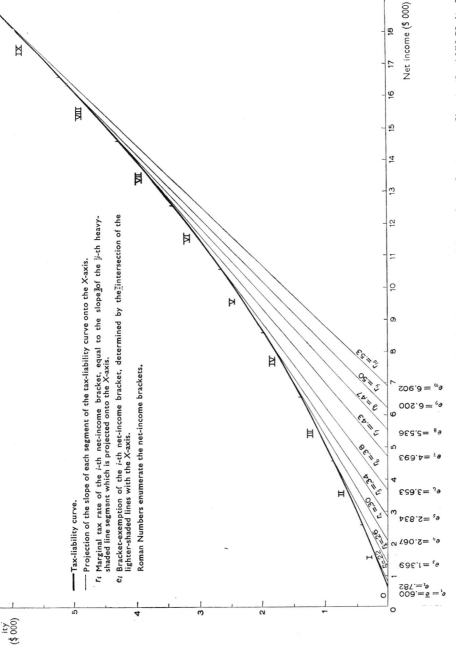

PLATE VII. Tax liability and bracket-exemptions for single persons with no dependents according to the 1959 United States federal income tax with a continuing exemption of $600

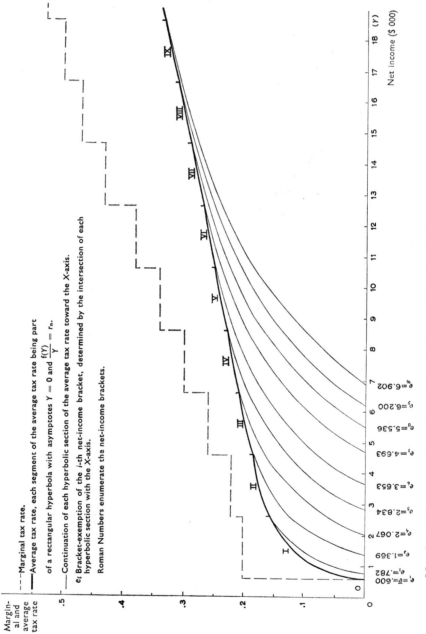

PLATE VIII. Marginal and average tax rates and bracket-exemptions for single persons with no dependents according to the 1959 United States federal income tax with a continuing exemption of $600

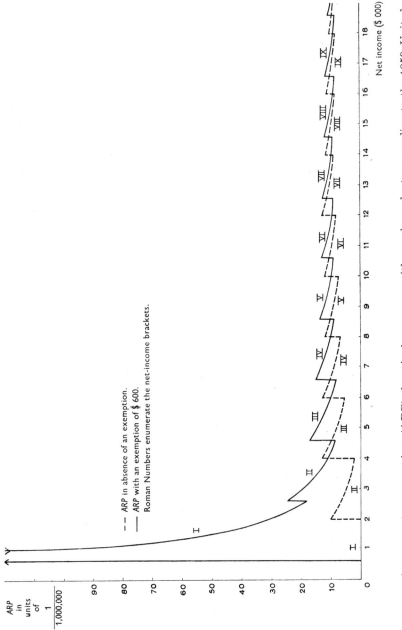

PLATE IX. Average-rate progression (ARP) for single persons with no dependents according to the 1959 United States federal income tax in absence of an exemption and with an exemption of $600.

proportional taxation to the progressive income tax. Only, instead of dealing with a single proportional tax, we now deal with a whole series of connected proportional-tax bands. Hence, the average tax rate becomes a series of connected sections of successive rectangular hyperbolas, each of which has the asymptotes $Y = 0$ and $f(Y)/Y = r_n$ (see the heavy-shaded curves in Plates VI and VIII). Since the marginal rates increase from bracket to bracket, as income increases, the upper asymptote $(f(Y)/Y = r_n)$ of each rectangular hyperbola exceeds that of the preceding one. Therefore, the average tax rate increases in the form of a series of connected rising arcs, as is shown by the heavy-shaded curves in Plates VI and VIII. The lighter-shaded curves are the continuation of each hyperbola towards the X-axis; their intersection with the axis equals, again, the bracket-exemption. For example, the second highest heavy-shaded arc represents the average rate for the IX-th income class, that is, for net income of $16,000–18,000 in Plate VI and for net income of $16,600–18,600 in Plate VIII. The continuation of the hyperbola towards the X-axis (second lighter-shaded curve from the right) intersects the axis at $5,600 and $6,200, respectively, which is the bracket-exemption for the IX-th income class without a statutory exemption, and with a (statutory) continuing exemption of $600, respectively.

In general, for any given net income level within a given net-income bracket, the slope of the average rate schedule will be steeper (that is, the average-rate progression (ARP) will be larger), the higher the marginal rate of that bracket and the larger its bracket-exemption.[16] Of course, as a rule, we are concerned with changes in the whole marginal-rate structure. These will affect all marginal rates and, usually, at the same time most bracket-exemptions (see Section E of this chapter). However, our analysis in terms of the marginal (bracket-) rate and of the bracket-exemption enables us to concentrate on any single bracket and to determine the effects on the average rate and on the ARP of that bracket, while disregarding

---

[16] This is best demonstrated by the income levels where two net-income brackets join. At these levels, the ARP jumps up. These jumps are shown in *Plate IX.*

all the other brackets.[17] Thus, a complex problem can be reduced to a set of simple components which, thereafter, can easily be combined to provide the whole picture. This technique is used in the following section, where we analyze the impact on the average tax rate and the ARP of changes in the size of the continuing exemption and in the marginal-rate structure.

E. The Impact on the Average Tax Rate and the Average-Rate Progression (ARP) of Changes in the Size of the Continuing Exemption and in the Marginal-Rate Structure

1. CHANGES IN THE SIZE OF THE CONTINUING EXEMPTION[18]

Increasing the (statutory) continuing exemption by a certain amount is equivalent to shifting upward the net-income brackets (including the "zero bracket") by the amount of the increment in the exemption. Correspondingly, all bracket-exemptions are increased by exactly the same amount as is the statutory exemption. Thus, the new set of hyperbolic curves which now form the average tax rate cut the X-axis further to the right than the rectangular hyperbolas of the previous set, that is, each new hyperbola is lower and steeper than its previous counterpart with the same asymptotes. The result is a reduction in the average tax rate and an increase in the average-rate progression (ARP), for any given level of net income, wherever the old hyperbolas are replaced by the new ones with the same asymptotes. However, each new hyperbola, because of the shift in the net-income brackets, will also replace a section of a hyperbola whose upper asymptote is higher, where the exemption shifts the net-income bracket. Over this range, the ARP is likely to be reduced.[19] These relationships can be visualized by comparing Plate vi with Plate viii. However, they are most

---

[17] Of course, the preceding brackets are not really disregarded, but the effects of their rate changes are summarized in the new bracket-exemption of the bracket under consideration.

[18] These cover also the change from a "zero exemption" to a positive exemption.

[19] This analysis corresponds exactly to "case i" (where the exemption cuts across a taxable-income bracket) of our previous approach (Sections B and C of this chapter).

clearly seen in Plate IX where the ARP resulting from the income tax with a continuing (statutory) exemption of $600 is superimposed on the ARP which would result in absence of a statutory exemption. Notice that the exemption increases the ARP over those income ranges where the old and new net-income brackets co-incide and reduces the ARP over the ranges where the exemption shifts the net-income bracket limit (except for the transition from the first to the second bracket).

Utilizing our analysis of proportional taxation, we are able to make some more specific statements with regard to the ARP. Given a proportional tax, an increase in the exemption by a given proportion increases the ARP schedule by the same proportion.[20] The same holds for each proportional-tax band of our transformation over the income range where the new net-income bracket co-incides with the old one. However, notice that a given increase in the statutory exemption increases all bracket-exemptions by the same *absolute* amount, that is, it increases each successive bracket-exemption by a smaller proportion than the preceding one. Thus, over the stated income range, the relative increase in the ARP schedule becomes smaller and smaller for successive income brackets. The percentage impact of the continuing exemption (or of a change in its size, as the case may be) on the ARP can be measured, for each income bracket, by the ratio of the new bracket-exemption divided by the old bracket-exemption, or by the ratio of the old bracket-exemption divided by the new one, depending on whether the relative impact of the exemption is to be expressed as a percentage of the old or the new ARP schedule.[21] Table 7 (see page 64) presents these ratios as well as the percentage increase in the ARP schedule, for each income bracket, due to an increase in the statutory exemption from zero to $600. The data are based on the 1959 United States federal income tax for single persons with no dependents. The close agreement between column (9) of Table 7 and column (7) of Table 5 is apparent (occasional slight differences are due to rounding). The tapering off of

---

[20] See Chapter II, Section D.

[21] Of course, this is true only with regard to that part of each net-income bracket where the new bracket co-incides with the old one, that is, where the exemption does not shift the bracket.

the impact of the continuing exemption on progressivity is clearly demonstrated.

2. CHANGES IN THE RATE STRUCTURE

There exists an infinite variety of possible changes in the marginal rate schedule. However, most of those can be ruled out a priori. If the original tax structure was a sensible and accepted one, it is very unlikely that some marginal rates would be shifted in opposite directions, that is, that some marginal rates would be increased while some other rates would simultaneously be reduced.[22] Furthermore, if we accept tax criterion II,[23] changes in the marginal rates are limited to the extent that no marginal rate can be increased to the point where it would exceed the next bracket rate after its increase; and no marginal rate can be reduced to the point where it would fall below the preceding marginal rate after its reduction. Since the highest marginal rate cannot exceed 100% (by tax criterion III)[24] and the lowest rate cannot be below zero, this is a strong limitation.

Given these two limitations, increases in (or reduction of) the marginal rate can be classified into three major categories: (1) proportional changes in all marginal rates, (2) changes of successive marginal rates at an increasing rate, and (3) changes of successive marginal rates at a decreasing rate. The most popular changes are either a change of all rates by a constant proportion (1), or a change of all rates by a constant number of percentage points (3). "Mixed changes," involving more than one category, have to be broken down into "pure" sections. To each section, the appropriate type of analysis can then be applied.

(1) Proportional changes in all marginal rates.[25]

A proportional increase in all marginal rates does not affect the

---

[22] Even in absence of more fundamental reasons, sheer political pressure in a democracy is likely to prevent this type of rate adjustment.

[23] See Chapter I, Section B.

[24] *Idem.*

[25] For an incisive treatment of the material presented in this and the following paragraphs (§§ 1–3a) and proofs for the various propositions, see *Mathematical Appendix* to Chapter III.

TABLE 7. *Bracket-exemptions for single persons with no dependents under the 1959 United States federal income tax, assuming either no statutory exemption or a continuing statutory exemption of $600—and percentage impact of the statutory exemption*

No. of income bracket	Taxable-income bracket ($000)	Marginal (bracket) rate v_n	Bracket-exemption given a $0 statutory exemption e_n	Bracket-exemption given a $600 statutory exemption e'_n	ARP for $600 exemption as percentage of ARP for $0 exemption (%)	Change in ARP as percentage of ARP for $0 exemption (%)	ARP for $0 exemption as percentage of ARP for $600 exemption (%)	Change in ARP as percentage of ARP for $600 exemption (%)
(1)	(2)	(3)	(4)	(5)	(6)	(7)	(8)	(9)
1	0—2	.20	0	600	—	—	0	100.0
2	2—4	.22	182	782	429.7	329.7	23.3	76.7
3	4—6	.26	769	1369	178.0	78.0	56.2	43.8
4	6—8	.30	1467	2067	140.9	40.9	71.0	29.0
5	8—10	.34	2234	2834	127.3	27.3	78.6	21.4
6	10—12	.38	3053	3653	119.6	19.6	83.6	16.4
7	12—14	.43	4093	4693	114.6	14.6	87.2	12.8
8	14—16	.47	4936	5536	112.1	12.1	89.2	10.8
9	16—18	.50	5600	6200	110.7	10.7	90.4	9.6
10	18—20	.53	6302	6902	109.5	9.5	91.3	8.7
11	20—22	.56	7036	7636	108.5	8.5	92.2	7.8
12	22—26	.59	7797	8397	107.7	7.7	92.9	7.1
13	26—32	.62	8677	9277	106.9	6.9	93.6	6.4
14	32—38	.65	9754	10354	106.1	6.1	94.2	5.8
15	38—44	.69	11391	11991	105.3	5.3	95.0	5.0
16	44—50	.72	12750	13350	104.7	4.7	95.5	4.5
17	50—60	.75	14240	14840	104.2	4.2	96.0	4.0
18	60—70	.78	16000	16600	103.7	3.7	96.4	3.6
19	70—80	.81	18000	18600	103.3	3.3	96.8	3.2
20	80—90	.84	20214	20814	103.0	3.0	97.1	2.9
21	90—100	.87	22621	23221	102.6	2.6	97.4	2.6
22	100—150	.89	24360	24960	102.5	2.5	97.6	2.4
23	150—200	.90	25756	26356	102.2	2.2	97.8	2.2
24	200+	.91	27670	28270	102.1	2.1	97.9	2.1

Notes:

In absence of a statutory exemption, the net-income brackets and the taxable-income brackets are identical; in case of a continuing statutory exemption ($600), the amount of this exemption has to be added to the lower and upper bracket limit of each taxable-income bracket in order to derive the corresponding net-income bracket. Therefore, the percentage impact of the statutory exemption (columns (7) and (9)) refers various bracket-exemptions (see Plate x). Thus it is equivalent to a change in the series of proportional tax rates by the same relative amount, and our analysis of rate changes under proportional taxation can be applied. The conclusion is that both the average rate schedule and the ARP schedule are increased (i.e., shifted upward) by the same proportion as the marginal rate schedule. Similarly, a reduction of the whole marginal rate schedule by a given proportion will result in a reduction (i.e., shifting downward) of both the average rate schedule and the ARP schedule by the same proportion.

(2) Changes of successive marginal rates at an increasing rate.

An increase of successive marginal rates at an increasing rate will increase all bracket-exemptions except the first one (i.e., the statutory exemption) (see Plate x). Since the statutory exemption is not affected, the net-income brackets will remain unchanged. However, the increase in the bracket-exemption tends to reduce the impact of the rate increase on the average rate and to reinforce its impact on progressivity, as measured by the ARP, within each bracket. Thus, over the range of the first bracket, the average rate and the ARP will increase in proportion to the relative increase in the first marginal rate, whereas over the range of every other bracket, the average rate will increase by a smaller proportion than

---

only to those income ranges for which the net-income brackets for zero and for $600 statutory exemptions co-incide, for example, $600–2,000, $2,600–4,000, etc.

(6) The new ARP, within the common net-income bracket-range, as percentage of the old ARP is given by $100 \, (e'_n/e_n)$, that is, (6) $= 100 \, [(5)/(4)]$.

(7) The impact of the continuing statutory exemption on the ARP within the common net-income bracket-range, measured as a percentage of the old (lower) ARP, is given by col. (6)–100.

(8) The old ARP, within the common net-income bracket-range, as percentage of the new ARP is given by $100 \, (e_n/e'_n)$, that is, (8) $= 100 \, [(4)/(5)]$.

(9) The impact of the continuing statutory exemption on the ARP, measured as a percentage of the new (higher) ARP, is given by 100–col. (8).

— Not defined (division by zero).

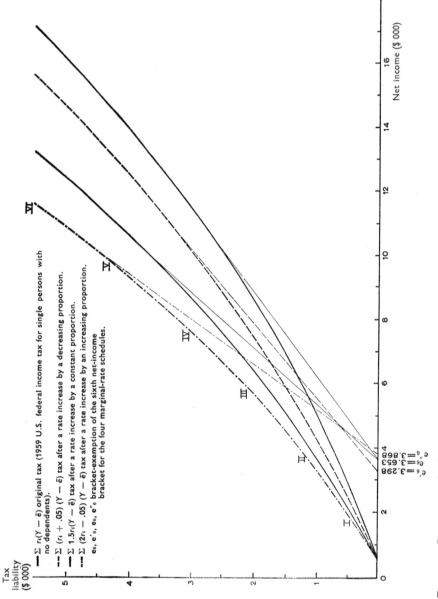

PLATE x. Impact on the bracket-exemption of increases in successive marginal rates by a decreasing, constant,

the corresponding marginal rate and the ARP, by a larger proportion.[26]

(3) Changes of successive marginal rates at a decreasing rate.

An increase of successive marginal rates at a decreasing rate will reduce all bracket-exemptions except the first one (i.e., the statutory exemption) (see Plate x). Since the statutory exemption is not affected, the net-income brackets will remain unchanged. The reduction in the bracket-exemption tends to reinforce the impact of the rate increase on the average rate and to reduce its impact on the ARP. Over the first bracket range, both the average tax rate and the ARP will increase in proportion to the relative increase in the first marginal rate, for any given income level, whereas over each of the higher bracket ranges, the average tax rate will increase by a larger proportion than the corresponding marginal rate and the ARP will either increase by a smaller proportion or may even decline.[27]

(3a) Special case: changing all marginal rates by a constant number of percentage points.

This is but a special case of a change at a decreasing rate. However, this case merits some special attention for three reasons: (1) such "changes across the board" are among the most widely used rate adjustments, (2) they represent the limiting case where the "marginal-rate progression" remains unchanged,[28] and (3) some more specific statements can be made in this case with regard to the ARP. More specifically, in case of a rate increase across the board, the ARP schedule will be shifted upward within each income bracket, but by a smaller proportion than the marginal bracket rate. Furthermore, the proportion by which the ARP

---

[26] Within each bracket range, the proportion by which the average rate is increased increases as income increases, but always remains below the proportion by which the marginal rate is increased.

[27] Within each bracket range, the proportion by which the average rate is increased declines as income increases, but always remains above the proportion by which the marginal rate is increased.

[28] See R. A. MUSGRAVE AND THUN TIN, "Income Tax Progression, 1929–48," *Journal of Political Economy*, LVI (December, 1948), p. 504.

schedule is shifted upward declines for each successive bracket.

This indicates that the ARP schedule could decline only in extreme cases, when the marginal rates are increased at a rate which declines very fast, indeed.

CHAPTER IV

CHANGES IN THE SIZE OF THE CONTINUING EXEMPTION VERSUS CHANGES IN THE MARGINAL-RATE STRUCTURE AS A MEANS OF ADJUSTING TAX REVENUE[1]

Whenever revenue is to be adjusted, the whole tax system has to be considered. The decision which taxes to adjust is not independent of the decision how to adjust each tax. Thus, we have to begin our analysis with a simplifying assumption. We shall assume that a certain adjustment of revenue is to be achieved by changes in the income tax and that the magnitude of the adjustment (which is "allocated" to the income tax rather than to other taxes) does not depend on the particular type of income-tax change selected. Given this assumption, we shall analyze changes in the size of the continuing exemption as compared with rate changes.

There exist four fundamental differences between changes in revenue by means of adjusting the size of the exemption and changes in revenue by means of adjusting the rate structure. They are: (1) Differences with regard to the "coverage" of income-tax payers.[2] (2) Differences with regard to the determination of the

---

[1] For a discussion of this problem with regard to small incomes see WILLIAM VICKREY, "Adjustment of Income Tax Schedules for Small Incomes," in *Federal Tax Policy for Economic Growth and Stability;* Papers Submitted by Panelists Appearing Before the Subcommittee on Tax Policy; Joint Committee on the Economic Report (Washington: U.S. Government Printing Office, 1956), pp. 347–353. A closely related analysis may be found in WILLIAM VICKREY, "Rate Reduction or Increased Exemptions," *National Tax Association;* 1954 Proceedings of the Forty-Seventh Annual Conference on Taxation (Sacramento: 1955), pp. 288–295.

[2] "Coverage," as used here, is defined by the tax laws and regulations which determine under which conditions there arises an actual tax liability. Hence "coverage" is closely related to, but nevertheless distinct from, the actual number of taxpayers. For example, a change in "coverage" may merely affect the number of potential (future) taxpayers, leaving the number of actual current taxpayers unchanged. Of course, it is more likely to change both.

pattern of adjustment. (3) Differences with regard to the impact of the adjustment on the average tax rate and the average-rate progression (ARP). (4) Differences with regard to incentive effects. A fifth difference, though not a fundamental one, is administrative in nature. Furthermore, some consideration should be given to the reversibility of the adjustment. Even though these last two considerations are not of a purely analytical nature, they will be briefly discussed at the end of this chapter for the sake of completeness. The main emphasis in our analysis will be on incentive-to-work effects.

A. Differences with Regard to the Coverage of Income-Tax Payers

A change in the size of the exemption will change the coverage of taxpayers and, therefore, tends to change the number of active current taxpayers as well as the number of potential future taxpayers. An adjustment in the rate structure, on the other hand, leaves the coverage of taxpayers unaffected. Whether it is desirable to have the coverage of taxpayers expand and contract with statutory changes in revenue cannot be decided purely on the basis of economic reasoning.[3] The answer to this question depends on the rationale which justifies the exemption in the first place. Administrative feasibility and convenience should be considered, too. (These are briefly discussed in Section E of this chapter.)

B. Differences with Regard to the Determination of the Pattern of Adjustment

Given the tax brackets, the marginal-rate structure, and the distribution of income,[4] the magnitude of the contemplated change

---

[3] We consider here the problem of statutory changes in revenue as contrasted with changes arising due to "built-in flexibility" and the like.

[4] If additional exemptions are granted for dependents, the aged, the blind, etc., complete knowledge of the income distribution classified by all these categories is needed.

in revenue determines uniquely the new level of the exemption which, in turn, determines uniquely the new average rate schedule and ARP schedule.[5]

However, given the tax brackets, the size of the exemption, and the income distribution, there exist a large number of possible changes in the marginal-rate structure which will result in the same change of total revenue but in different average rate and ARP schedules. Thus, first we have to choose a specific type of change of the marginal-rate structure (for example a change across the board). Only thereafter will the exact level of the new marginal rate schedule (as well as that of the average rate and ARP schedules) be uniquely determined by the size of the revenue-change. In other words, a decision has to be made as to the new type, or shape, of marginal-rate structure; only then can the level of this rate structure be uniquely determined. This additional decision, however, carries also certain benefits. It leaves us some discretionary power with regard to the shape of the new average rate schedule and ARP schedule.

C. Differences with Regard to the Impact of the Adjustment on the Average Tax Rate and the Average-Rate Progression (ARP)

As mentioned before, changes in the size of the exemption, by changing the coverage of the tax, are likely to introduce some new active taxpayers by increasing their average tax rate from zero to some positive value, or to remove some taxpayers by reducing their average rate to zero. Thus the (new) coverage of taxpayers for changes in the size of the exemption differs from the (unchanged) coverage for rate adjustments. For strict comparison, we have to restrict ourselves to those persons who will be active taxpayers in both cases. It should be noted, however, that an increase in revenue places a lighter additional tax burden on the previous taxpayers, if achieved by means of changes in the size of the exemption, and a reduction in revenue gives less relief to the remaining

---

[5] This as well as the following proposition is evident from the discussion in the *Mathematical Appendix* to Chapter III.

taxpayers. This is due to the change in the coverage of taxpayers.

From our previous analysis it is known that a change in the size of the exemption will shift the average tax rate by absolute (and even more so relative) amounts which become smaller and smaller as income increases (see Table 5, column (5)). Therefore, an increase (reduction) in the size of the exemption will reduce (increase) the proportion of total tax revenue collected from the lower income groups. In many countries, by far the major part of total income (national income, as well as net income) accrues to the low and medium income groups. Where this is the case, the bulk of the additional tax relief, or of the tax burden, as the case may be, will fall on those income groups, whereas taxpayers with high incomes will be affected to a negligible degree. (For example, see Table 15, columns (2) and (4).) Furthermore, progressivity will increase (decline), over most income ranges as the size of the exemption increases (declines). However, at least for some income ranges the ARP is likely to move in the opposite direction. The impact of a change in the size of the exemption on the ARP will taper off, as income increases, becoming negligible for high incomes. This gradual tapering off is shown in Table 5, column (7), and also in Table 7, columns (7) and (9).

Rate changes permit us to place the bulk of the revenue adjustment on any particular income group, or to spread it out in proportion to the allocation of the previous tax burden. The following holds with regard to the three basic categories of rates changes which were discussed in the preceding chapter: (1) A proportional change in all marginal rates spreads the revenue adjustment evenly, that is, in proportion to the allocation of the previous tax burden. (2) Increasing (reducing) successive marginal rates at an increasing rate tends to increase (reduce) the proportion of total tax revenue collected from the middle and upper income groups, whereas (3) increasing (reducing) them at a decreasing rate tends to increase (reduce) the proportion of total tax revenue collected from the lower income groups (however, as a rule to a lesser degree than changes in the size of the exemption). This latter type of rate change seems to be the one which is most widely used.

Rate adjustments tend to affect tax progressivity in the opposite direction from adjustments in the size of the exemption; increases in revenue result in increased progressivity, as measured by the ARP, and reductions in revenue in reduced progressivity.

D. Differences with Regard to Incentive-to-Work Effects[6]

The allocation of time between work and leisure depends on two important economic variables: (1) the level of the individual's income, and (2) the "price of leisure," that is, the amount of income foregone per unit of time (given a certain pattern of intensity of work). The higher the level of his real disposable income, ceteris paribus, the larger the amount of leisure a person is likely to consume, granted that leisure is not an inferior good.[7] Similarly, the higher the "price of leisure," that is, the higher the net marginal rate

---

[6] For a general discussion of incentive effects, see LIONEL ROBBINS, "On the Elasticity of Demand for Income in Terms of Effort," *Economica*, x (June, 1930), reprinted in *Readings in the Theory of Income Distribution* (Philadelphia: Blakiston Co., 1946), pp. 237–244; DUNCAN BLACK, *The Incidence of Income Taxes* (London: Macmillan and Co., Ltd., 1939), Chap. XII, pp. 157–167; OTTO VON MERING, *The Shifting and Incidence of Taxation* (Philadelphia: Blakiston Co., 1942), Chap VI, Sec. 2; RICHARD GOODE, "The Income Tax and the Supply of Labor," *Journal of Political Economy*, LVII (October, 1949); GERSHON COOPER, "Taxation and Incentive in Mobilization," *Quarterly Journal of Economics*, LXVI (February, 1952); GEORGE F. BREAK, "Income Taxes, Wage Rates, and the Incentive to Supply Labor Services," *National Tax Journal*, VI (December, 1953); CARL S. SHOUP, "Taxation and Fiscal Policy," in *Income Stabilization for a Developing Democracy*, ed. MAX F. MILLIKAN (New Haven: Yale University Press, 1953), pp. 262–277; GEORGE F. BREAK, The Effects of Taxation on Work Incentives," in *Federal Tax Policy for Economic Growth and Stability*, Papers Submitted by Panelists Appearing Before the Subcommittee on Tax Policy, Joint Committee on the Economic Report (Washington: U.S. Government Printing Office, 1956), pp. 192–199, and CLARENCE D. LONG, "Impact of the Federal Income Tax on Labor Force Participation," *ibid.*, pp. 153–166. For an excellent summary treatment, see RICHARD A. MUSGRAVE, *The Theory of Public Finance* (New York, Toronto, London: McGraw-Hill Book Co., Inc., 1959), pp. 232–248.

[7] For the characteristics of "inferior goods," see J. R. HICKS, *Value and Capital* (2nd ed.; Oxford: Clarendon Press, 1946), Chap. 2. Clearly, leisure is not an inferior good.

of remuneration for work at a given income level,[8] the smaller will be the amount of leisure consumed. The income tax tends to reduce both the level of real disposable income and the net marginal rate of remuneration.[9] The net effect of the tax on the amount of leisure consumed can be analyzed with the traditional Hicksian indifference curve apparatus, being broken down into the "income effect" and the "substitution effect".[10] The general conclusions of this approach can be summarized in the following way:

> The tax-induced reduction in aggregate income will normally be followed by a decreased demand for leisure, since leisure can be considered to be complementary to other objects of consumption. But by *lowering* the cost of leisure . . ., the tax, through its "substitution effect," will tend to increase the quantity demanded. The net effect of these opposing incentives will vary with the relative income and price elasticities of the demand for leisure.[11]

---

[8] The "net marginal rate of remuneration" is the "take-home" rate of remuneration for the marginal unit of work (measured in dollars per hour, per day, etc.). The "gross marginal rate of remuneration" is the marginal rate of remuneration prior to deduction of the income-tax liability. DUNCAN BLACK (*op. cit.*, p. 159) calls them net and gross rate of remuneration, respectively. However, under a progressive income tax, there exists no unique net rate of remuneration for any given gross rate. In some cases, such as overtime pay, the gross rate itself may depend on the marginal unit of work. Generally, if w denotes the gross marginal rate of remuneration per unit of time and r_n the marginal rate of the income tax, then the net marginal rate of remuneration, w_n, i.e., the price of leisure (where leisure is measured in the same time units) is given by:

$$w_n = (1 - r_n)w.$$

[9] After the government has spent the tax money, real disposable income of some people may be unchanged or may even have increased. However, here we are concerned with the incentive-to-work effects of income taxation. Different patterns of government spending are likely to create different types of incentive effect. Thus, it seems appropriate to apply a "partial analysis" approach to the problem under consideration.

[10] For an exposition of the Hicksian indifference curve analysis, see HICKS, *loc. cit.*; also J. R. HICKS AND R. G. D. ALLEN, "A Reconsideration of the Theory of Value," *Economica*, I, II new series (February, May, 1934).

[11] HASKELL P. WALD, "The Classical Indictment of Indirect Taxation,"

Various economists, using different analytical approaches, have all reached the same conclusion of indeterminacy,[12] that is, they all agree that the tax may increase the total amount of labor supplied, leave it unchanged, or reduce it, depending on the preference patterns of the individuals with regard to income and leisure.

Through the development of a modified and refined indifference curve approach, we shall try to extend the analysis of the effects of income taxation on incentives to work in order to derive a number of significant conclusions even in absence of the knowledge of the precise income and price elasticities of the demand for leisure. Our conclusions fall into two broad categories. For the first set of conclusions, one has to establish whether the income and price elasticities of the demand for leisure tend to rise, remain constant, or fall with increases in the level of income. Such knowledge can be established more readily and with a greater degree of confidence than the precise magnitudes of these elasticities. A carefully designed sample survey of planned adjustments in leisure could possibly provide some of this information.[13] The second set of conclusions does not require any knowledge of either the

---

Quarterly Journal of Economics, LIX (August, 1945), p. 583. For a similar treatment of the problem, utilizing the indifference-curve approach, see VON MERING, *op. cit.*, pp. 111–114; also BLACK, *op. cit.*, pp. 157–167.

[12] E.g., COOPER, *loc. cit.*; also ROBBINS, *loc. cit.*, and GEORGE F. BREAK, *Income Taxes, Wage Rates, and the Incentive to Supply Labor Services.*

[13] Needless to say, any such survey would require a great deal of planning and would encounter a large number of serious problems which lie beyond the scope of this study. One possible approach would attempt to establish the adjustment in leisure (or work) in response to an actual or hypothetical pure change in income, or in the price of leisure, at various income levels in terms of $O–X$ %, $X–X'$ %, etc. The questions would have to be as complete and specific as possible (e.g. planned changes in overtime, extra, or part-time, work, unpaid vacation, etc.). In the United States, similar surveys have been carried out quite successfully in the field of planned saving and consumption adjustments of consumers in response to expected income changes (Survey Research Center of the University of Michigan, "Annual Survey of Consumer Finances," *Federal Reserve Bulletin*. Published annually since 1947, these surveys usually begin with the June issue of the Bulletin and are continued in subsequent issues).

magnitudes or the direction of changes of the income and price elasticities.

The two sets of major conclusions can be summarized in the following way: (1) Without any knowledge of the actual income and price elasticities of the demand for leisure, merely using varying combinations of assumptions as to whether these elasticities rise or fall with increases in the level of income, we can determine from the tax structure, for certain combinations, whether an increase in the exemption will cause the lower income groups to decrease their work by a larger proportion (or increase it by a smaller proportion) than the higher income groups, or vice versa: the same information can be obtained with respect to a decrease in the rate scale of a specified type. (2) In comparing equal-revenue exemption increases and rate reductions (for the United States federal income tax), we can determine, without any recourse to either the magnitudes or the direction of changes of the income and price elasticities, whether certain income groups are likely to reduce their work more (or increase it less) in relative and absolute terms, if one system of tax reduction is chosen rather than the other.

Before we develop our approach in order to reach the specified conclusions, a short discussion and clarification of the concept of "income elasticity of the demand for leisure" seems appropriate.[14] We noticed that the net incentive-to-work effect depends on the "relative income and price elasticities of the demand for leisure."[15] In this context, most writers refer to the "income elasticity of the demand for leisure" as if this was a uniquely defined concept. However, certain conceptual difficulties are likely to arise. One is likely to agree that the demand for leisure (like the demand for any commodity) is best related to "real disposable income," but "real disposable income" can have different meanings. For any given set of prices, we could consider "real disposable income" in terms of

---

[14] The following clarification of this concept represents my response to some thought-provoking questions raised by Professor Abba Lerner in connection with an earlier draft of this study.

[15] WALD, *loc. cit.*, p. 583.

"general purchasing power (Marshall's 'money'),"[16] irrespective of the allocation of this "general purchasing power" among different commodities. Viewed in this way, "real disposable income" could be measured by the amount of disposable income which would accrue to the individual if no leisure whatsoever was consumed; that is, this "general purchasing power" includes, in any particular case, both leisure actually consumed and "expenditure" (on goods, services, and saving) actually made. This "general purchasing power" (as we shall call it henceforth) is indicated by OR_0 in Figure 7,

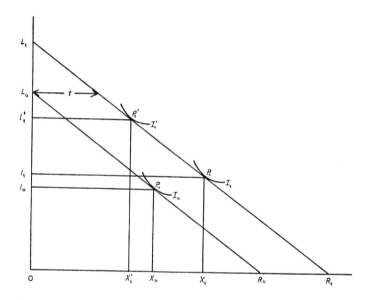

Fig. 7. Changes in "general purchasing power," in "real disposable money income," and in the demand for leisure, due to the abolition of a poll-tax (t)

where leisure is measured along the vertical axis and earned disposable income along the horizontal axis, and where L_0R_0 is the

---

[16] J. R. HICKS, *Value and Capital*, Chap. II, § 4, p. 33. The analysis in terms of "general purchasing power" follows closely Hicks's Chapter II.

"budget line" representing all possible allocations of the "general purchasing power" OR_0 between "expenditure" and leisure.[17] Assume now that a poll-tax of the amount $t = R_1 - R_0$, which had been levied previously, is refunded. The refund increases "general purchasing power" from OR_0 to OR_1, that is, by a ratio of t/OR_0, where t measures the tax relief. If I_0 and I_1 are the indifference curves tangent to L_0R_0 and L_1R_1 at P_0 and P_1 respectively, then the demand for leisure is increased from l_0 to l_1, that is, by a ratio of $l_1 - l_0/l_0$. Thus the "real income elasticity of the demand for leisure," when measured in terms of "general purchasing power" is:

$$\varepsilon_R = \frac{l_1 - l_0}{l_0} \bigg/ \frac{t}{OR_0}, ^{18} \quad \text{or simply,} \quad \varepsilon_R = \frac{\Delta l}{l} \bigg/ \frac{t}{OR}.$$

Usually, however, the income elasticity is defined with regard to relative changes in observed (or theoretically observable) income rather than with regard to Hicksian "general purchasing power," that is, that part of "general purchasing power" which is taken in form of leisure is excluded. In case of Figure 7, this "real disposable money income" elasticity, as we may call it, is given by:

$$\varepsilon_X = \frac{l_1 - l_0}{l_0} \bigg/ \frac{X_1 - X_0}{X_0}, \quad \text{or simply,} \quad \varepsilon_X = \frac{\Delta l}{l} \bigg/ \frac{\Delta X}{X}.$$

ε_X will be greater than, equal to, or smaller than, ε_R, depending on whether ε_R is greater than, equal to, or smaller than one, provided neither leisure nor "expenditure" (on goods, services, and saving)

---

[17] For the sake of simplicity, Figure 7 is drawn as if either a proportional income tax without exemption (not indicated in diagram) or no income tax whatsoever was levied. With a progressive income tax, the "budget line" would turn into a series of connected line segments with successively increasing slopes (e.g., see WALD, *loc. cit.*, p. 585, Figure III, also pp. 587–588, and p. 589, Figures IV and V).

[18] In this exposition, the simple point-elasticity formulae are used. A commonly used arc-formula is:

$$\varepsilon_R = \frac{l_1 - l_0}{l_1 + l_0} \bigg/ \frac{t}{OR_0 + OR_1}$$

is an inferior good (that is, provided $\varepsilon_X \geq 0$).[19] However, the difference between the two concepts of income elasticity is best demonstrated by the extreme and unrealistic case where "expenditure" (on goods, services, and saving) is assumed to be an inferior good, leisure being a superior good. In Figure 7, indifference curve I_1' and equilibrium point P_1' represent this case. ε_R would be much greater than one, whereas ε_X would be negative. "General purchasing power" would be increased by t, as previously, but observed "real disposal money income" would be reduced from X_0 to X_1'. Since the demand for leisure is increased from l_0 to l_1, leisure would appear to be an inferior rather than a superior good, if observed "real disposable money income" were taken as our measure of real income. This paradoxical result is due to the fact that the latter measure of real income leaves out of account one important commodity which contributes to real income, namely leisure. Actually, neither leisure nor "expenditure" (on goods, services, and saving) is likely to be an inferior good and, probably, the two measures of real income elasticity of the demand for leisure will not differ widely.

---

[19] A geometrical proof of this proposition is as follows:

Given the point of tangency of an indifference curve (P_0) with the old budget line (L_0R_0), and given the new budget line (L_1R_1) representing a higher level of "general purchasing power," the point on the new budget line which yields $\varepsilon_R = 1$ is given by the intersection of this budget line (P_1) with a line through the origin and P_0. In this case,

$$\frac{l_1 - l_0}{l_0} = \frac{R_1 - R_0}{R_0} = \frac{X_1 - X_0}{X_0} \text{, and therefore } \varepsilon_R = \varepsilon_X = 1.$$

$\varepsilon_X \geq 0$ implies $l_1 \geq l_0$ and $X_1 \geq X_0$, for increases in "general purchasing power." As we move along the budget line L_1R_1 to the right of P_1 (keeping within the area where $l_1 \geq l_0$), $X_1 - X_0$ increases whereas $R_1 - R_0$ remains constant. Thus, ε_X declines faster than ε_R, and hence $\varepsilon_X < \varepsilon_R < 1$. Similarly, if we move along the budget line L_1R_1 to the left of P_1 (keeping within the area where $X_1 \geq X_0$), $X_1 - X_0$ declines whereas $R_1 - R_0$ remains constant. Thus, ε_X increases faster than ε_R, and hence $\varepsilon_X > \varepsilon_R > 1$.

In the following analysis, we shall use a third concept of real disposable income elasticity of the demand for leisure which, for the sake of simplicity, will be called "income elasticity."[20] With regard to the relative change in income, it represents a mixture between ε_R and ε_X, having the same numerator, t, as ε_R and the same denominator, X_0, as ε_X for its income-fraction. Using the symbols of Figure 7,

$$\varepsilon = \frac{l_1 - l_0}{l_0} \bigg/ \frac{t}{X} , \quad \text{or simply,} \quad \varepsilon = \frac{\Delta l}{l} \bigg/ \frac{t}{X} .$$

In other words, ε allows for the full increment to "real income" (in terms of "general purchasing power") irrespective of whether this increment is realized in form of leisure or in form of "expenditure" (on goods, services, and saving), but expresses this increment as a percentage only of the original "real income" (in terms of "real disposable money income") which was taken in form of "expenditure." ε will always be smaller than ε_R; it will also be smaller than ε_X, provided neither leisure nor "expenditure" is an inferior good. However, ε does not represent a simple change of scale of ε_R, unless the proportion of "general purchasing power" allocated to "expenditure" remains constant for all levels of "general purchasing power."

What is the purpose of introducing the concept of the "income elasticity" ε? Our analysis will prove the operational usefulness of this concept. However, the essential features can be mentioned before-hand. Empirically, the indifference maps are unknown. Thus, we know neither the "new" quantity of leisure demanded (l_1) nor the "new" level of observable "real disposable money income" (X_1). Such is the nature of the complete indeterminacy which arises with respect to incentive effects and which has been mentioned before: l_1 is unknown as long as ε_X is unknown (which, incidentally, contains l_1). Chances for exact empirical determination of ε_X are slim; therefore, this approach tends to yield no results in addition to that of "indeterminacy."

---

[20] "Impact elasticity of income" might be a more appropriate term, but sounds a bit too clumsy.

On the other hand, the relative change of real disposable income used for ε(that is t/X_0) can be computed without any knowledge of the "new" quantity of leisure demanded and can throw some additional light on our problem. The relative change of "general purchasing power" (t/R_0) could be computed, but not without great difficulties especially under a progressive income-tax system. Furthermore, in order to compute it, one has to decide what constitutes "zero consumption of leisure," a very awkward matter, indeed.[21] Thus, the concept of ε will prove the most useful one for our analysis and will be employed throughout. The results reached are likely to be very similar to those that would result from the use of ε_R, since our technique is based on the direction of changes of ε rather than on its absolute value.

With these preliminaries out of the way, we shall now develop our approach with regard to changes in the size of the exemption and changes in the tax-rate structure. A comparison of those alternative methods of revenue adjustment will emphasize certain differences with regard to their effect on incentives to work.

(1) Impact of a change in the size of the exemption on incentives to work.
A change in the size of the exemption does not affect the taxable-income brackets or the tax-rate schedule. However, it shifts the net-income brackets corresponding to given taxable-income brackets by an amount equal to the change in the size of the exemption.[22] For example, assume that the taxable-income brackets range over $2,000 each and that the marginal tax rates for the first

---

[21] This is the same as deciding what constitutes the maximum amount of work possible. The routine answer of 24 hours a day will not be satisfactory, since a certain number of hours has to be allocated to sleep, consumption of meals, etc., not by choice, but rather by necessity. The fruitlessness of pursuing this very far and the arbitrariness of any decision is pointed out by ALFRED MARSHALL in his short discussion of the concepts of "productive consumption" (of which our "productive consumption" of leisure is a part). ALFRED MARSHALL, *Principles of Economics* (8th ed.; London: Macmillan and Co., Ltd., 1920), Bk. II, Chap. 3, § 2.

[22] For a definition and utilization of the concepts of "taxable-income brackets" and "net-income brackets," see *Chapter III*, Section A and *Mathematical Appendix* to Chapter III.

three brackets are 20%, 30%, and 40% respectively. If the exemption is now increased from $500 to $1,000, the only change is an upward shift in the net-income brackets by $500. This can be seen from Table 8, comparing columns (1) and (2). It is immediately apparent that disposable income is increased for all income levels exceeding $500. Thus, granted that leisure is not an inferior good, the income effect will tend to increase the amount of leisure consumed for all taxpayers.[23] What about the substitution effect? The net marginal rate of remuneration (that is, the "price of leisure") remains unchanged for any income level falling in segments of "old" and "new" net-income brackets that correspond to the same taxable-income bracket as before—for instance, the segment $3000–4500 in the third line, first two columns, of Table 8.[24] The net marginal rate of remuneration will be changed only for the income ranges over which the new exemption shifts the net-income brackets[25]—for instance, the range $4500–5000 in the third line, first two columns, of Table 8. Within these ranges, the net marginal rate of remuneration will be increased to the level obtaining in the next lower "old" net-income bracket. Thus, within these ranges, both the income effect and the substitution effect are operative and

TABLE 8. *Impact of an increase in the size of the exemption on the net-income brackets (a numerical example)*

Net-income brackets for an exemption of		Taxable-income brackets	Marginal rates	Tax liability at the upper bracket limit
$500 (1)	$1000 (2)	$ (3)	% (4)	$ (5)
0– 500	0–1000	0	0	0
500–2500	1000–3000	0–2000	20	400
2500–4500	3000–5000	2000–4000	30	1000
4500–6500	5000–7000	4000–6000	40	1800

[23] That is, for all persons who were active taxpayers while the exemption was $500.

[24] These segments are given by the right hand figure in column 1 with the left hand figure in column 2.

[25] Given by linking the two right hand figures (or the two left hand figures) in columns 1 and 2.

work against each other. The net result cannot be determined unless the relevant income and substitution elasticities are known. This is as far as the traditional analysis goes. From here we shall now extend and develop it.

The income elasticity (ε) has been defined previously as $(\varepsilon = \triangle l/l)$: (t/X), where t is the increment (or decrement) accruing to "general purchasing power" due to a change in the tax liability and X is "disposable money income." Therefore $\triangle l/l = \varepsilon(t/X)$, that is, the relative change in the amount of leisure demanded due simply to a change in disposable income is equal to the product of our income elasticity times the relative change in disposable income. This expression can thus be used as a measure of the income effect and will be called the "relative income effect."[26]

Similarly, the price elasticity of the demand for leisure (ε_p) is defined as $\varepsilon_p = (\triangle l/l)/(\triangle P/P)$ and hence $\triangle l/l = \varepsilon_p(\triangle P/P)$, that is, the relative change in the amount of leisure demanded due simply to a change in the price of leisure is equal to the product of the price elasticity times the relative change in the price of leisure. This expression can be used as a measure of the substitution effect and will be called the "relative substitution effect."[27]

Given a change in the size of the exemption, the relative change of disposable income and of the price of leisure can be computed for every net income level. Then, if we know whether the elasticities are positively or negatively correlated with the level of income, we can derive some specific conclusions. We shall now carry out this analysis.

---

[26] Actually, the income effect measures the absolute change in the amount of leisure demanded $(\triangle l)$ and, thus, is equal to l times the "relative income effect." Since the "original" amount of leisure demanded can be considered known, the relative income effect can always be transformed into an absolute income effect. Our analysis will be carried out mainly in terms of relative changes in the amount of leisure demanded.

[27] Actually, the substitution effect measures the absolute change in the amount of leisure demanded $(\triangle l)$ and, thus, is equal to l times the "relative substitution effect." Since the "original" amount of leisure demanded can be considered known, the relative substitution effect can always be transformed into an absolute substitution effect. Our analysis will be carried out mainly in terms of relative changes in the amount of leisure demanded.

First, let us consider the relative change in disposable income resulting from a given change in the size of the exemption. In certain preceding sections, such an analysis has been carried out with regard to changes in disposable income measured as a percentage of net income rather than of disposable income.[28] The conclusion was that the change in disposable income, as a percentage of net income, falls over most income ranges with an increase in net income, but is likely to rise within each range where the new exemption shifts the net-income bracket. Similar conclusions hold with regard to the percentage change in disposable income, that is, the change in disposable income measured as a percentage of disposable income rather than of net income. For any given change in the size of the exemption, this percentage change in disposable income will decline with an increase in net income over the range within each net-income bracket, where the "old" and the "new" brackets co-incide. Over the ranges where the new exemption shifts the net-income bracket, the percentage change in disposable income is likely to increase with an increase in net income. Thus, we have to ascertain whether the general trend is one of decline or of increase. In other words, the question arises whether the percentage change in disposable income shows a tendency to decline consistently from, say, one bracket limit to the next one, as income increases. It can be shown that such a consistent decline, while by no means necessary, is at least very likely to occur in case of most actual income-tax structures.[29] This outcome is the more likely, the smaller the size of the incre- ments to the marginal rate, the closer the top marginal rate to 0.5, and the wider the tax brackets. Successive declines in the marginal- rate increments and a successive widening of the income brackets tend to increase the likelihood of this outcome. Many modern income-tax structures contain most of these specific features. A good instance is the United States federal income tax, which will be used as an example in our analysis.[30] Table 9 shows the abso-

---

[28] See especially Chapter III, Sections B, C, and E § 1; also *Mathematical Appendix* to Chapter III.

[29] The conditions for such a decline are provided in the *Mathematical Appendix* to Chapter IV.

[30] The United States federal income tax contains most of the features

lute and the percentage increase in disposable income of single persons and married couples with no dependents, and of married couples with two dependents, that would result from an increase in the United States income tax exemption from $600 to $700 per capita. It illustrates the steady decline in the percentage increase of disposable income, t/X, with increases in the level of net income.

Given that the income elasticity of the demand for leisure were positively correlated with the level of income, the rate at which this elasticity increases with income would determine whether the relative income effect, $\varepsilon(t/X)$, following a given increase in the exemption, would tend to decline, remain constant, or increase, as the level of income increases. This in turn would determine what would happen to the relative change in the amount of leisure demanded, as net income increases, since $\varepsilon(t/X) = \triangle l/l$. In case of the United States federal income tax, it can be seen from Table 9, columns (4), (7), and (10), that the relative income effect would decline with increases in the level of income at least over the lower income ranges, unless the income elasticity were to increase at a fairly substantial rate over those ranges. Consequently, given that the income elasticity of the demand for leisure would remain fairly constant or would even decline with increases in the level of income, for a certain change in the size of the exemption, the size of the relative income effect would tend to decline steadily as we move from lower to higher income levels. That is, the relative change in the amount of leisure demanded would be smaller at higher income levels than at lower ones.

Let us now turn to the substitution effect. It is important to keep in mind that, given a change in the size of the exemption, the substitution effect affects but a limited number of taxpayers, that is, only those who are moved into another income bracket. Thus, our present analysis refers only to these taxpayers. The

---

mentioned as contributing to a steady decline in the percentage change of disposable income. See U.S. *Internal Revenue Code: 1954 Code Edition* (Chicago, New York, Washington: Commerce Clearing House, Inc., 1954), Sec. 1.

TABLE 9. *Absolute and percentage increase in "disposable income" of single persons and married couples with no dependents and of married couples with two dependents, assuming an increase in the United States federal income tax exemption from $600 to $700 per capita*

Net income ($)	Single person no dependents			Married couple no dependents			Married couple 2 dependents		
	Disposable income ($)	Absolute increase in disposable income ($)	Percentage increase in disposable income (%)	Disposable income ($)	Absolute increase in disposable income ($)	Percentage increase in disposable income (%)	Disposable income ($)	Absolute increase in disposable income ($)	Percentage increase in disposable income (%)
(1)	(2)	(3)	(4)	(5)	(6)	(7)	(8)	(9)	(10)
1,000	920	20	2.17	1,000	—	—	1,000	—	—
2,000	1,720	20	1.16	1,840	40	2.17	2,000	—	—
3,000	2,512	22	0.87	2,640	40	1.52	2,880	80	2.78
4,000	3,292	22	0.67	3,440	40	1.16	3,680	80	2.17
5,000	4,056	26	0.64	4,240	40	0.94	4,480	80	1.79
8,000	6,220	30	0.48	6,584	44	0.67	6,848	88	1.29
10,000	7,564	34	0.45	8,112	52	0.64	8,408	88	1.05
15,000	10,552	47	0.44	11,740	60	0.51	12,100	120	0.99
25,000	15,204	59	0.39	18,276	76	0.42	18,732	152	0.81
50,000	23,612	72	0.30	30,408	118	0.39	31,116	236	0.76
100,000	33,202	87	0.26	47,224	144	0.30	48,088	288	0.60
500,000	70,726	91	0.13	96,452	182	0.19	97,544	364	0.37
1,000,000	130,522	—[a]	—[a]	141,452	182	0.13	142,544	364	0.26

[a] Maximum effective rate limitation 87 per cent of taxable income as defined by the tax law.

Note:

Columns (4), (7), (10) are computed by dividing columns (3), (6), (9) by 1/100 of columns (2), (5), (8) respectively.

Sources:

Columns (1), (3), (6), and (9) are taken from Staff of the Joint Committee on Internal Revenue Taxation, *Alternative Plans for Reducing the Individual Income Tax Burden* (Washington: U.S. Government Printing Office, 1956), plan 1, pp. 2–3. The computation of columns (2), (5), and (8) is based on the provisions of the *1954 U.S. Internal Revenue Code*.

relative change in the price of leisure, $\triangle P/P$, for those taxpayers, is:

(1)
$$\frac{\left(\begin{array}{c}\text{``new'' net marginal rate}\\ \text{of remuneration}\end{array}\right) - \left(\begin{array}{c}\text{``old'' net marginal rate}\\ \text{of remuneration}\end{array}\right)}{\text{``old'' net marginal rate of remuneration}}$$

or, for large differences, using an arc formula,

(2)
$$\frac{2\left[\left(\begin{array}{c}\text{``new'' net marginal rate}\\ \text{of remuneration}\end{array}\right) - \left(\begin{array}{c}\text{``old'' net marginal rate}\\ \text{of remuneration}\end{array}\right)\right]}{\text{``old'' + ``new'' net marginal rate of remuneration}} \, ^{[31]}.$$

Thus, the relative change in the price of leisure depends on the magnitude of the "old" marginal tax rate and on the difference between it and the adjacent marginal tax rate. In most countries with a progressive income tax, the marginal tax rates increase steadily by a uniform number of percentage points, except for the first marginal rate or the first two rates, and sometimes the very top rates.[32] In other words, the net marginal rate of remuneration

---

[31] Given an increase in the size of the exemption, the percentage increase of the net marginal rate of remuneration for those, who are moved into a lower income bracket, is given by:

(a) $$\frac{w_{n-1} - w_n}{w_{n-1}} = \frac{[(1-r_{n-1}) - (1-r_n)]w}{(1-r_{n-1})w} = \frac{r_n - r_{n-1}}{1-r_{n-1}},$$

where w denotes the "gross marginal rate of remuneration;" w_i, the "net marginal rate of remuneration" (i.e. the marginal wage rate after income taxation) for income falling within the i-th tax bracket; and r_i, the corresponding top marginal tax rate. The corresponding arc-formula is:

$$\frac{2(w_{n-1} - w_n)}{w_{n-1} + w_n} = \frac{2(r_n - r_{n-1})}{(1-r_n) + (1-r_{n-1})} = \frac{2(r_n - r_{n-1})}{2 - (r_n + r_{n-1})}.$$

From these expressions we see that constant rate increments result in a steady rise of the percentage increase of the price of leisure from bracket to bracket.

[32] The difference between zero and the lowest marginal rate is usually much greater than that between any two of the succeeding marginal rates. (E.g., see U.S. Internal Revenue Code; 1954 Code Edition, Sec. 1). Examples of fairly constant increases in the marginal rates are found in the German

declines by a uniform number of dollars per income bracket, as income rises. In the fractions above, the numerator tends to remain constant, while the denominator falls from bracket to bracket, as income rises. Hence, the general tendency of the percentage increase in the price of leisure, associated with a given change in the size of the exemption, is to increase over most of the income range, as income increases. However, this tendency, though widespread, is by no means inherent in the tax structure of the progressive income tax. It depends completely on the rate structure of the tax, that is, on the regularity or irregularity with which the marginal rates increase by a constant number of percentage points from bracket to bracket. These general features as well as certain irregularities are illustrated in Table 10, showing the percentage increase in the price of leisure for single persons within the relevant income ranges for an increase in per capita exemptions of the United States federal income tax from $600 to $700. Note the rather erratic rate changes over the taxable-income brackets of $12,000–14,000, $14000,–16,000, $16,000–18,000 and the tapering off of the rate increase over the highest three brackets. They make for a rather irregular behavior of the percentage change of the price of leisure. Incidentally, the former of those two irregularities in the rate schedule can hardly be justified on any rational basis. In spite of these irregularities, there appears a fairly clear-cut division between the low and medium income levels (up to taxable income of about $38,000) on the one hand, and the higher income levels on the other. The percentage increase of the price of leisure for the former group is well below ten per cent for an increase in the exemption from $600 to $700. For the latter group, it is at least ten per cent and mostly much in

---

income taxes from 1920–1925, the English "super-tax" for 1920/21, the U.S. "surtax" from 1918–1926, the French income tax from 1914–1917 and from 1920–1925 (see KARL BRÄUER, *Umrisse und Untersuchungen zu einer Lehre vom Steuertarif* (Jena: Gustav Fischer, 1927), pp. 166–168, 170, 172–175); also in the income tax for many Swiss "cantons" (see PIERRE FOLLIET, *Les Tarif d'Impôts* (Lausanne: Librairie Payot, 1947), pp. 471–473, 479). Note, however, such examples of unsystematic rate progression as in the Danish income tax of 1922, the French income tax of 1944, the British income tax of 1941 (see FOLLIET, *op. cit.*, pp. 483, 486–488).

TABLE 10. *Percentage increase of the net marginal rate of remuneration for single persons with no dependents due to an increase in the per capita exemption of the United States federal income tax from $600 to $700*

Net-income range ($)	Taxable-income range for an exemption of $600 ($)	Taxable-income range for an exemption of $700 ($)	Marginal tax rate applied to col (2) (%)	Marginal tax rate applied to col (3) (%)	Reduction in marginal tax rate (col. (4) - col. (5))	Percentage increase of "net marginal rate of remuneration," using reg. formula	Percentage increase of "net marginal rate of remuneration," using arc-formula
(1)	(2)	(3)	(4)	(5)	(6)	(7)	(8)
0.6–0.7	0.0–0.1	0	20	0	20	25.0	24.7
2.6–2.7	2.0–2.1	1.9– 2.0	22	20	2	2.6	2.5
4.6–4.7	4.0–4.1	3.9– 4.0	26	22	4	5.4	5.3
6.6–6.7	6.0–6.1	5.9– 6.0	30	26	4	5.7	5.6
8.6–8.7	8.0–8.1	7.9– 8.0	34	30	4	6.1	5.9
10.6–10.7	10.0–10.1	9.9– 10.0	38	34	4	6.4	6.2
12.6–12.7	12.0–12.1	11.9– 12.0	43	38	5	8.8	8.4
14.6–14.7	14.0–14.1	13.9– 14.0	47	43	4	7.5	7.3
16.6–16.7	16.0–16.1	15.9– 16.0	50	47	3	6.0	5.8
18.6–18.7	18.0–18.1	17.9– 18.0	53	50	3	6.4	6.2
20.6–20.7	20.0–20.1	19.9– 20.0	56	53	3	6.8	6.6
22.6–22.7	22.0–22.1	21.9– 22.0	59	56	3	7.3	7.1
26.6–26.7	26.0–26.1	25.9– 26.0	62	59	3	7.9	7.6
32.6–32.7	32.0–32.1	31.9– 32.0	65	62	3	8.6	8.2
38.6–38.7	38.0–38.1	37.9– 38.0	69	65	4	12.9	12.1
44.6–44.7	44.0–44.1	43.9– 44.0	72	69	3	10.7	10.2
50.6–50.7	50.0–50.1	49.9– 50.0	75	72	3	12.0	11.3
60.6–60.7	60.0–60.1	59.9– 60.0	78	75	3	13.6	12.7
70.6–70.7	70.0–70.1	69.9– 70.0	81	78	3	15.8	14.6
80.6–80.7	80.0–80.1	79.9– 80.0	84	81	3	18.7	17.1
90.6–90.7	90.0–90.1	89.9– 90.0	87	84	3	23.1	20.7
100.6–100.7	100.0–100.1	99.9–100.0	89	87	2	18.2	16.7
150.6–150.7	150.0–150.1	149.9–150.0	90	89	1	10.0	9.5
200.6–200.7	200.0–200.1	199.9–200.0	91	90	1	11.1	10.5

Note:

All dollar figures are in 000's of dollars. For the computation of columns (7) and (8), the following formulae have been used, respectively:

$$100 \frac{r_n - r_{n-1}}{100 - r_{n-1}} \quad \text{and} \quad 100 \frac{2(r_n - r_{n-1})}{200 - (r_n + r_{n-1})},$$

where r_n is the top marginal rate applicable to the given net income, as listed in column (4), and r_{n-1} the adjacent lower rate, as listed in column (5).

excess of this figure. The largest percentage change of the price of leisure, however, is the one affecting the very lowest income group, that is, the one that drops out of the universe of taxpayers.

Given this pattern of percentage changes of the price of leisure, and given also the direction of changes in the price elasticity of the demand for leisure as income increases, there would follow certain conclusions with regard to the direction of change of the relative substitution effect, due to a certain increase in the exemption. If the individual price elasticities, ε_p, of the demand for leisure were negatively correlated with income, the relative substitution effect (that is, the relative change in the amount of leisure demanded due to a change in the price of leisure) might be stronger, equal, or weaker at high income levels than at medium and low income levels, depending on the rate at which the price elasticity declines as income increases. We could only be certain that the relative substitution effect would be strongest at the very lowest income level, because of the very large percentage change in the price of leisure at that level.

If, however, the individual price elasticities of the demand for leisure were positively correlated with the level of income (or remained fairly constant with increases in the level of income), more specific conclusions would result. In this case, the relative substitution effect would be much stronger at high income levels than at medium and low ones (yet it might be fairly strong at the very lowest income level), since both ε_p and $\triangle P/P$ would be, in general, greater at higher income levels.

The analysis of the relative income effect, resulting from an increase in the exemption, can now be combined with that of the relative substitution effect. We shall not summarize all possible combinations, but rather limit ourselves to the assumption that the income elasticity of the demand for leisure remains fairly constant or declines with increases in the level of income, whereas the price elasticity remains fairly constant or increases with the level of income.[33] In this case, the majority of individuals who are affected

---

[33] This particular case has been singled out, not because it is the most likely one (after all, likelihood can be established only on the basis of empirical evidence), but rather because it yields the most clear-cut results. The reader can easily trace other combinations. In those cases, the results will be less clear-cut.

solely by the income effect tend to reduce the amount of work done by a smaller proportion at higher, than at lower, income levels. Of those affected by the substitution effect, the tendency toward more work, from an increase in the exemption, would be stronger on this count at the higher income levels. Therefore, of those affected by both the income effect and the substitution effect, those with lower incomes (except the very lowest) are likely to reduce their work by a larger proportion, or increase it by a smaller proportion, than will those with higher incomes. However, little can be said about the very important and numerous group of those with the very lowest incomes, that is, those who would move out of the first statutory income bracket.

In case of changes in the size of the exemption, there exists a built-in limitation of the substitution effect. If, for an increase in the exemption, the substitution effect outweighs the income effect at a given income level, the individual will increase the amount of work done. This will soon move him back into the higher income bracket where the substitution effect is suspended and only the income effect is operating. Thus, only small marginal increases in the amount of work done by a person can be expected in this case. (Of course, these small amounts could add up to a substantial aggregate.)

Before we present an estimate of the proportion of taxpayers affected by both the income effect and the substitution effect, we shall summarize the results of the preceding analysis.

We noticed that the relative income effect, that is, the relative change in the amount of leisure demanded due to a pure change in "general purchasing power," is equal to the product of the income elasticity of the demand for leisure times the relative change in disposable income. Using symbols, $\triangle l/l = \varepsilon(t/X)$. In case of the United States federal income tax, we saw that t/X declines as income increases, for a given increase in the exemption. Thus, if ε remains fairly constant, or even more so if ε declines, as income increases, the relative income effect $\triangle l/l$ will decline as income increases.

Similarly, we noticed that the relative substitution effect, that is, the relative change in the amount of leisure demanded due to a pure change in the price of leisure, is equal to the product of the price elasticity of the demand for leisure times the relative change in the price of leisure. Using symbols, $\triangle l/l = \varepsilon_p(\triangle P/P)$. In case of the United States federal income tax, we saw that $\triangle P/P$, if it changes at all, increases with the level of income, for a given increase in the exemption, except for the very lowest income group, and with some exceptions farther up the income scale. Thus, if ε_P remains fairly constant, or even more so if ε_p increases, as income increases, the relative substitution effect $|\triangle l/l|$ will, in general, increase with increases in income.[34]

Given these assumptions about ε and ε_p, of those affected by both income effect and substitution effect, those with lower incomes will experience a stronger relative income effect and a weaker relative substitution effect than those with higher incomes. There- fore, the former will tend to increase the amount of leisure demanded by a larger proportion, or reduce the amount of leisure demanded by a smaller proportion, than the latter. Thus, the first conclusion stated at the outset of this analysis has been demonstrated.

An attempt will now be made to determine the proportion of taxpayers affected by *both* the income effect and the substitution effect and their distribution among the various income brackets. The proportion and distribution of these taxpayers depends, of course, on the specific tax structure and income distribution of the country. Thus, conclusions can be drawn on the basis of case studies, which are of a limited, rather than of a general, nature. For illus- trative purposes, such an estimate has been carried out for the year 1951 for the United States, assuming that the per capita exemption had been \$700 rather than \$600 (see Table 11).[35] A number of rather strong assumptions had to be made in order to carry out this estimate, the major one being that of uniform distribution of income tax returns within each income range for which the data were

---

[34] In case of a tax reduction, the relative (as well as the absolute) substitu- tion effect is negative. Thus it is, of course, its absolute value which increases with increases in income.

[35] The estimate is based on U.S. Treasury Department, Internal Revenue Service, *Statistics of Income for 1951* (Washington: U.S. Government Printing Office, 1955), Pt. 1, Table 9, p. 64.

TABLE 11. *Number and percentage of taxable returns shifted into a lower income bracket because of an increase of the per capita exemption from $600 to $700—an estimate for the United States for 1951*

| | Assuming that no income-splitting is granted | | Income splitting granted for joint returns | |
| | Number of returns | | Number of returns | |
(1)	in absolute figures (2)	as % of total (3)	in absolute figures (4)	as % of total (5)
1 Exemption	13,382,138	100.00	13,382,138	100.00
Returns shifted into zero bracket	506,096	3.78	506,096	3.78
Returns shifted into zero or first bracket	840,979	6.28	840,979	6.28
Returns shifted into any lower bracket	884,797	6.61	884,797	6.61
2 Exemptions	11,706,929	100.00	11,706,929	100.00
Returns shifted into zero bracket	426,286	3.64	426,286	3.64
Returns shifted into zero or first bracket	983,808	8.40	850,544	7.27
Returns shifted into any lower bracket	1,373,918	11.74	921,910	7.87
3 Exemptions	7,591,747	100.00	7,591,747	100.00
Returns shifted into zero bracket	489,403	6.45	489,403	6.45
Returns shifted into zero or first bracket	1,078,529	14.21	668,602	8.81
Returns shifted into any lower bracket	1,357,927	17.89	698,868	9.21
4 Exemptions	5,652,533	100.00	5,652,533	100.00
Returns shifted into zero bracket	603,969	10.68	603,969	10.68
Returns shifted into zero or first bracket	1,041,393	18.42	717,096	12.67
Returns shifted into any lower bracket	1,245,017	22.03	751,715	13.30
5 Exemptions	2,348,080	100.00	2,348,080	100.00
Returns shifted into zero bracket	459,142	19.56	459,142	19.56
Returns shifted into zero or first bracket	673,389	28.68	508,950	21.68
Returns shifted into any lower bracket	765,671	32.23	527,631	22.47

TABLE 11. *(continued)*

(1)	Assuming that no income-splitting is granted Number of returns		Income splitting granted for joint returns Number of returns	
	in absolute figures (2)	as % of total (3)	in absolute figures (4)	as % of total (5)
6 Exemptions or more	912,795	100.00	912,795	100.00
Returns shifted into zero bracket	252,328	27.64	252,328	27.64
Returns shifted into zero or first bracket	324,719	35.57	270,543	29.64
Returns shifted into any lower bracket	368,295	40.35	283,689	31.08
1 Exemption or more	41,594,222	100.00	41,594,222	100.00
Returns shifted into zero bracket	2,737,224	6.58	2,737,224	6.58
Returns shifted into zero or first bracket	4,942,817	11.88	3,856,714	9.27
Returns shifted into any lower bracket	5,995,625	14.41	4,068,610	9.78

Source:

U.S. Treasury Department, Internal Revenue Service, *Statistics of Income for 1951* (Washington: U.S. Government Printing Office, 1955), Pt. 1, Table 9, p. 64.

given.[36] The margin of error cannot be determined, but it is, without doubt, very substantial. Therefore, this estimate can serve only as an illustration and indication of the order of magnitude involved. It should be noted that all figures refer to the number of tax returns rather than to the number of taxpayers. If we were to assume that

---

[36] Other important assumptions made, were:

1. Application of the "standard deduction" of 10% for incomes up to $10,000 and allowance of the maximum "standard deduction" of $1,000 for incomes in excess of $10,000.

2. Allocation of joint returns in the following way:

All returns with three or more exemptions (other than age or blindness) were assumed to be joint returns, using income splitting. The remainder of the joint returns were allocated to returns with two exemptions, this allocation

all joint returns represented two income recipients, the number of persons shifted into the zero bracket by the $100 increase in the per capita exemption would be 4,888,293, the number shifted into either the zero or the first bracket would be 6,521,871, and the total number shifted into a lower bracket would be 6,862,882. Of course, only a limited number of joint returns represents two separate income recipients. On the other hand, the figures in our table tend to have a downward bias, since 2,645,981 extra exemptions for age and blindness have not been taken into consideration.[37] An alternate estimate has been made, assuming that no income splitting was permitted for joint returns. A comparison of those two estimates (Table 11) illustrates strikingly to what extent the number of tax-payers who experience a substitution effect depends on the specific tax structure as well as the income distribution. Our estimate indicates that this number may be fairly substantial even for relatively small changes in the size of the exemption. It will be the greater, the larger the average number of exemptions per tax return granted by the law, the more narrow the range of the income brackets, and the higher the concentration of tax returns at the lower bracket limits.

(2) Impact of a change of the tax-rate schedule on incentives to work.
   The analysis turns now to a demonstration of the second theorem stated at the outset of this section: a comparison of equal-revenue exemption increases and rate reductions with respect to their effects on incentives to work, for certain income groups. As a first step, the effect of a change in the tax-rate schedules must be analyzed. Later (§ 3), the actual comparison will be carried out. The preceding

---

being carried out separately for each income interval, or bracket, given in the source.

   3. For the tabulation of "six or more" exemptions, the average number of exemptions was computed for each income interval and uniformly applied to this interval.

   4. No attempt was made to allocate the extra exemptions for age and blindness, so that their effect is not accounted for in this estimate.

   [37] Exemptions for age (over 65) and blindness are specified in the *U.S. Internal Revenue Code, 1954 Code Edition*, Sec. 151 (c) and (d).

discussion of exemption changes has provided the foundation for the present analysis of rate changes. Therefore, the present treatment can be somewhat more concise.

There are two categories of rate changes: (1) "corrective" rate changes, that is, adjustments of one or several marginal tax rates so as to smooth the overall rate structure, and (2) "fundamental" rate changes, that is, adjustments of all marginal tax rates.[38] We shall be concerned with the latter category only.

All such reductions of the rate schedule will increase the disposable income of all taxpayers. The income effect will therefore tend to reduce the amount of work done. On the other hand, all such reductions of the rate schedule will also increase the net marginal rate of remuneration for all taxpayers, so that the substitution effect will tend to increase the amount of work done. All taxpayers are affected by both the income effect and the substitution effect which tend to counteract each other. As pointed out previously, the net effect on incentives to work is undetermined, unless the exact income and price elasticities of the demand for leisure are known. However, we shall use here the same technique as before in order to derive some more specific information. We shall compute the percentage changes of disposable income, t/X, and the percentage changes of the price of leisure, $\triangle P/P$, for different income levels in order to derive the maximum amount of knowledge possible and to facilitate comparison with the preceding case.

First, let us analyze the percentage changes of disposable income due to a given change in the rate schedule. It is most convenient to start this analysis with "across-the-board" rate changes, because the results from this case can easily be generalized.[39] Given a change of all marginal rates by a constant number of percentage points, the percentage change of disposable income, t/X, will increase with the level of income throughout.[40] This is illustrated in Table 12, showing

---

[38] For an extensive discussion and analysis of "fundamental" rate changes, see Chapter III, Section E, § 2; also *Mathematical Appendix* to Chapter III.

[39] The "across-the board" rate change is type (3a) ("special case"), discussed in Chapter III, Section E, § 2. Here we utilize the classifications which were established and justified there.

[40] Let c (a constant) be equal to the number of percentage points by which

the percentage increases of disposable income for selected income levels due to a reduction of all marginal tax rates of the 1959 United States income tax by two percentage points. As mentioned before, we are in a position to generalize our results. It can be shown that, if successively higher marginal rates are increased by an increasing number of percentage points, the percentage change of disposable income will always increase with increases in the level of net income.[41] Thus, in case of a "fundamental" change of the rate schedule we reach the following conclusions with regard to percentage changes of disposable income. The percentage change of disposable income will certainly increase with increases in the level of net income, if successively higher marginal rates are changed by an

---

all marginal rates are changed; i.e. $r'_i = r_i + c$, where all values are expressed in decimal fractions. The value of c is limited by the following conditions:
(1) $|c| \leq r_1$ for $c < 0$ (rate reductions),
(2) $c < 1 - r_n$ for $c > 0$ (rate increases).
The percentage change of disposable income, $\triangle X/X$, is given by:

$$\frac{\triangle X}{X} = \frac{c(\bar{e} - Y)}{Y - f(Y)} \lesseqgtr 0 \quad \text{for} \quad c \gtreqless 0.$$

Its rate of change is given by:

$$\frac{d\frac{\triangle X}{X}}{dY} = \frac{c[f(Y) - Yf'(Y) - \bar{e}(1 - f'(Y))]}{(Y - f(Y))^2} \lesseqgtr 0 \quad \text{for} \quad c \gtreqless 0.$$

Thus, the percentage change of disposable income due to an "across-the-board" rate change increases throughout as net income increases.

[41] (1) For rate reductions, let $0 > b_1 > b_2 > \ldots > b_n$, such that $0 \leq r_i + b_i < r_{i+1} + b_{i+1}$, where r_i denotes the marginal rate of the i-th tax bracket prior to the rate change, and b_i the rate change.

(2) For rate increases, let $0 < b_1 < b_2 < \ldots < b_n$, such that $r_i + b_i < r_{i+1} + b_{i+1} < 1$.

In general, let $r'_i = r_i + b_i$, where all values are expressed in decimal fractions. The percentage change of disposable income, $\triangle X/X$, is given by:

$$\frac{\triangle X}{X} = \frac{\sum_{i=1}^{n-1} b_i(Y_{i-1} - Y_i) + b_n(Y_{n-1} - Y)}{Y - f(Y)} \lesseqgtr 0 \quad \text{for} \quad b_i \gtreqless 0,$$

(continued on p. 99)

TABLE 12. *Absolute and percentage increase in "disposable income" of single persons and married couples with no dependents and of married couples with two dependents, due to a reduction of all marginal rates of the 1959 United States federal income tax by 2 percentage points*

Net income ($000's)	Single person no dependents			Married couple no dependents			Married couple 2 dependents		
	Disposable income ($)	Absolute increase in disposable income ($)	Percentage increase in disposable income (%)	Disposable income ($)	Absolute increase in disposable income ($)	Percentage increase in disposable income (%)	Disposable income ($)	Absolute increase in disposable income ($)	Percentage increase in disposable income (%)
(1)	(2)	(3)	(4)	(5)	(6)	(7)	(8)	(9)	(10)
1	920	8	0.87	1,000	—	—	1,000	—	—
2	1,720	28	1.63	1,840	16	0.87	2,000	—	—
3	2,512	48	1.91	2,640	36	1.36	2,880	12	0.42
4	3,292	68	2.07	3,440	56	1.63	3,680	32	0.87
5	4,056	88	2.17	4,240	76	1.79	4,480	52	1.16
8	6,220	148	2.38	6,584	136	2.07	6,848	112	1.64
10	7,564	188	2.49	8,112	176	2.17	8,408	152	1.81
15	10,552	288	2.73	11,740	276	2.35	12,100	252	2.08
25	15,204	488	3.21	18,276	476	2.60	18,732	452	2.41
50	23,614	988	4.18	30,408	976	3.21	31,116	952	3.06
100	33,202	1,988	5.99	47,224	1,976	4.18	48,088	1,952	4.06
500	70,762	9,988	14.12	96,452	9,976	10.34	97,544	9,952	10.20
1000	130,522	5,192[a]	3.98[a]	141,452	19,976	14.12	142,544	19,952	14.00

[a] Maximum effective rate limitation 87 per cent of taxable income as defined by the tax law.

Note:

Columns (4), (7), (10) are computed by dividing columns (3), (6), (9) by 1/100 of columns (2), (5), (8) respectively.

Sources:

Columns (1), (3), (6), and (9) are taken from Staff of the Joint Committee on Internal Revenue Taxation, *Alternative Plans for Reducing the Individual Income Tax Burden*, plan 7, pp. 14–15. The computation of columns (2), (5), and (8) is based on the provisions of the *1954 U.S. Internal Revenue Code*.

increasing, constant, or decreasing proportion, provided the proportion never decreases faster than an "across-the-board" rate change.[42] The faster the increase (or the slower the decline) of this proportion, the greater the increase in the percentage change of disposable income as the income level increases.

Given that the income elasticity of the demand for leisure remains fairly constant, or even increases, with increases in the level of income, the relative income effect due to a "fundamental" change in the marginal rate schedule increases steadily with the level of income. If the income elasticity of the demand for leisure were to decline with increases in the level of income, then it would depend on its rate of decline, whether the relative income effect would increase, remain constant, or decline, with increases in the level of income. Using symbols, since t/X increases with the level of income, the relative income effect $\triangle l/l = \varepsilon(t/X)$ will certainly increase with the level of income, if ε remains constant, or even more so if ε increases with increases in income. Even if ε declines with increases in the level of income, $\triangle l/l$ will increase with income, provided the rate of decline of ε is less than the rate of increase of t/X.

Now, let us discuss the percentage change in the price of leisure.

(continued from p. 97)
where Y_i denotes the upper bracket limit of the i-th net-income bracket. Its rate of change is given by:

$$\dfrac{d\,\dfrac{\triangle X}{X}}{dY} =$$

$$= \dfrac{(1 - f'(Y))\,[\sum\limits_{i=1}^{n-1} b_i(Y_i - Y_{i-1}) + b_n(Y - Y_{n-1})] - b_n(Y - f(Y))}{(Y - f(Y))^2} \lessgtr 0$$

$$\text{for } b_i \gtrless 0,$$

since $\quad |b_n(Y - f(Y))| >$

$$> |(1 - f'(Y))b_n Y| > |(1 - f'(Y)) [\sum\limits_{i=1}^{n-1} b_i(Y_i - Y_{i-1}) + b_n(Y - Y_{n-1})]|$$

$$\text{for } n > 1.$$

[42] Even if the proportion declines somewhat faster, the percentage change of disposable income will yet increase with increases in the level of income. However, as the rate of decline of the proportion is increased, a point will be reached where the percentage change of disposable income will decline at least over some income range.

Again, we shall start with an "across-the-board" rate change and then generalize our results. Given a change of all marginal rates by the same number of percentage points, the percentage change in the price of leisure will steadily increase over successive income brackets.[43] This result is illustrated in Table 13, showing the percentage increase of the price of leisure (net marginal rate of remuneration) due to a reduction of all marginal rates of the 1959 United States federal income tax by two percentage points.

The same result holds with regard to changes of successive marginal rates by an increasing number of percentage points. We reach the following conclusions concerning the percentage changes of the price of leisure due to "fundamental" changes in the marginal rate schedule. The percentage change of the price of leisure will steadily increase over successive income brackets, if successively higher marginal rates are changed by an increasing, constant, or decreasing proportion, provided this proportion never decreases much faster than an "across-the-board" rate change.[44] The faster

---

[43] Again, let c (a constant) be equal to the number of percentage points by which all marginal rates are changed and let the same limitations hold for the value of c as in footnote 40 on page 97. Then, the percentage change of the net marginal rate of remuneration, $(w'_n - w_n)/w_n$, is given by:

$$\frac{w'_n - w_n}{w_n} = \frac{[(1 - (r_n + c)]w - (1 - r_n)w}{(1 - r_n)w} = -\frac{c}{1 - r_n},$$

where w denotes the gross marginal rate of renumeration and r_n the top marginal rate expressed in decimals.

Since $r_1 < r_2 < \ldots < r_n < 1$, $\left|\dfrac{c}{1 - r_n}\right|$ will increase as income increases from bracket to bracket. I.e. the percentage change of the price of leisure will increase from bracket to bracket.

[44] There is no a priori reason why successively higher marginal rates should not be changed by a proportion that declines faster (even much faster) than an "across-the-board" rate change. However, in democratic countries this is not likely to happen. Whenever there exists a clash of interests, people try to establish a certain foothold for compromise. Concepts of maximization, minimization and equalization provide such footholds. In case of rate adjustments, the concept of equalization is the most likely one to be applied. Thus, equi-proportional rate changes, "across-the-board" rate changes, and

(continued on p. 102)

TABLE 13. *Percentage increase of the net marginal rate of remuneration for single persons and married couples due to a reduction of all marginal rates of the 1959 United States federal income tax by 2 percentage points*

Taxable-income range		Marginal tax rate		Percentage increase of the net marginal rate of remuneration	
single persons (000's $)	joint returns (000's $)	actual (%)	reduced (%)	reg. formula (%)	arc formula (%)
(1)	(2)	(3)	(4)	(5)	(6)
0—2	0—4	20	18	2.5	2.5
2—4	4—8	22	20	2.6	2.5
4—6	8—12	26	24	2.7	2.7
6—8	12—16	30	28	2.9	2.8
8—10	16—20	34	32	3.0	3.0
10—12	20—24	38	36	3.2	3.2
12—14	24—28	43	41	3.5	3.5
14—16	28—32	47	45	3.8	3.7
16—18	32—36	50	48	4.0	3.9
18—20	36—40	53	51	4.3	4.2
20—22	40—44	56	54	4.6	4.4
22—26	44—52	59	57	4.9	4.8
26—32	52—64	62	60	5.3	5.1
32—38	64—76	65	63	5.7	5.6
38—44	76—88	69	67	6.5	6.3
44—50	88—100	72	70	7.1	6.9
50—60	100—120	75	73	8.0	7.7
60—70	120—140	78	76	9.1	8.7
70—80	140—160	81	79	10.5	10.0
80—90	160—180	84	82	12.5	11.8
90—100	180—200	87	85	15.4	14.3
100—150	200—300	89	87	18.2	16.7
150—200	300—400	90	88	20.0	18.2
200+	400+	91	89	22.2	20.0

Note:

For the computations of col. (5) and col. (6), the following formulae were used, respectively:

$$-\frac{c}{100 - r_n} 100 \quad \text{and} \quad -\frac{2c}{2(100 - r_n) - c} 100,$$

where c is the across-the-board rate change in percentage points (in this case, $c = -2$), and r_n is the "original" top marginal rate applicable (col. (3)).

the increase (or the slower the decline) of this proportion, the greater the increase in the percentage change of the price of leisure between any two income brackets.

Given, the price elasticity of the demand for leisure is relatively constant, or is positively correlated, with income, then the relative substitution effect will increase from bracket to bracket, as income increases. If the price elasticity of the demand for leisure were negatively correlated with the level of income, then the relative substitution effect might increase, remain constant, or decline, with increases in the level of income, depending on the rate at which the price elasticity declines as income increases. Using symbols, since $\triangle P/P$ increases with the level of income, the relative substitution effect, $\triangle l/l = \varepsilon_p(\triangle P/P)$, will certainly increase with the level of income if ε_p remains constant, or even more so if ε_p increases, with increases in income. Even if ε_p declines with increases in the level of income, $\triangle l/l$ will yet increase with income, provided the rate of decline of ε_p is less than the rate of increase of $\triangle P/P$.

Now, let us combine the relative income effect and the relative substitution effect resulting from a reduction of all marginal rates of the 1959 United States federal income tax by two percentage points. If the income and price elasticities of the demand for leisure increase or remain constant (or decline at a sufficiently slow rate) with increases in the level of income, then both the relative income effect and the relative substitution effect will increase with the level of income. Table 14 gives the "equalizing ratios" between the income elasticity and the price elasticity of the demand for leisure, that is, the ratio between the elasticities which would result in an exact counterbalancing of the relative (and absolute) income effect by the relative (and absolute) substitution effect so that the amount of leisure demanded would remain unchanged. In this instance, the "equalizing ratios" fall from low to medium income levels and rise

(continued from p. 100)
changes of the tax liability by an equal proportion, are the most likely compromises. It is interesting to note that only the last two versions are represented among the 22 plans for reducing the individual income tax burden, prepared by the Joint Committee on Internal Revenue Taxation (op. cit.). (For equivalence of equi-proportional rate changes and changes of the tax liability by a constant proportion, see the treatment of "tax credits" in Chapter v.)

TABLE 14. *"Equalizing ratios" of $\varepsilon/\varepsilon_p$ (ratios of $\varepsilon/\varepsilon_p$ which would leave unchanged the amount of work done) for an "across-the-board" rate reduction of the 1959 United States federal income tax by 2 percentage points*

Net income	"Equalization ratios" of $\varepsilon/\varepsilon_p$[a]		
	Single person no dependents	Married couple no dependents	Married couple 2 dependents
(1)	(2)	(3)	(4)
1,000	2.87	—[b]	—[b]
2,000	1.53	2.87	—[b]
3,000	1.36	1.84	5.95
4,000	1.26	1.53	2.87
5,000	1.24	1.40	2.16
8,000	1.22	1.26	1.59
10,000	1.20	1.24	1.44
15,000	1.39	1.24	1.39
25,000	1.53	1.23	1.33
50,000	1.70	1.53	1.60
100,000	2.57	1.70	1.75
500,000	1.57	2.15	2.18
1,000,000	—[c]	1.57	1.58

[a] The "equalizing ratios" are derived from the equation which sets the relative income effect plus the relative substitution effect equal to zero, as follows:

$$\varepsilon \frac{t}{X} + \varepsilon_p \frac{\triangle P}{P} = 0, \quad \text{hence} \quad \frac{\varepsilon}{-\varepsilon_p} = \frac{\triangle P}{P} \bigg/ \frac{t}{X}.$$

(As a matter of convention, the absolute, rather than the arithmetic (negative), value of ε_p is considered in the table and related text). Thus, the figures in Table 14, columns (2), (3), and (4) are computed by dividing the figures in Table 13, column (5) which correspond to the given net income by the corresponding figures in Table 12, columns (4), (7), and (10) respectively.

[b] Those net income levels are tax exempt, hence there exist no "equalizing ratios" for them.

[c] This figure is omitted since it is not comparable, because of the effect of the maximum effective rate limitation of 87 per cent (see Table 12).

Sources:
Tables 12 and 13.

again towards the high income levels. Therefore, if, for example, both ε and $|\varepsilon_p|$ remained constant or increased (declined) with increases in the income level at the same rate, so that their ratio remained constant, then those with low and high incomes would increase their amount of leisure demanded by a smaller proportion (or reduce it by a larger proportion) than those with medium incomes.[45]

(3) Comparison of the impact of changes in the size of the exemption and of rate changes on incentives to work.

The following important differences should be kept in mind throughout our present comparison. "Fundamental" rate changes of the type considered here, when applied to a progressive income tax, give rise to definite and determined results with regard to the percentage changes of the price of leisure and of disposable income. On the other hand, the effects of changes in the size of the exemption on the percentage changes of the price of leisure and of disposable income depend on the particular bracket and rate structure of the income tax. The effects considered here are the ones typical for the present United States federal income tax. They may be adapted to other Western income taxes which are similar in structure.

In our comparison, we may be guided most conveniently by Tables 9 and 12, 10 and 13, respectively. For these two sets of tables to be strictly comparable, they would have to represent a change of revenue by exactly the same amount. The actual estimated changes of revenue for these tables are presented in Table 15. As shown there, the two types of tax reduction considered would probably have differed by less than three per cent ($72 million) in 1956. Thus, the tables can be considered roughly comparable.

A comparison of Tables 9 and 12 indicates that, given any set of income elasticities of the demand for leisure, adjustments of the size of the exemption (Table 9) will result in a stronger relative and absolute income effect for the low-income groups, a weaker relative and absolute income effect for the medium-income groups, and a

---

[45] Of course, these results would even be re-inforced if the income elasticity of the demand for leisure were to decline as income increased.

TABLE 15. *Estimated amount and distribution of an income tax reduction for the United States in 1956, assuming either an increase in per capita exemptions from $600 to $700, or a reduction of all marginal rates by 2 percentage points*

(1)	Tax reduction in millions of dollars		Percentage distribution of the tax reduction	
	assuming increase in the exemption	assuming tax-rate reduction	assuming increase in the exemption	assuming tax-rate reduction
	(2)	(3)	(4)	(5)
Income under $5,000	1,247	844	50.4	33.2
Income over $5,000	1,227	1,702	49.6	66.8
Total	2,474	2,546	100·0	100.0

Source:

Staff of the Joint Committee on Internal Revenue Taxation, *Alternative Plans for Reducing the Individual Income Tax Burden*, plan 1, p. 2, and plan 7, p. 14.

much weaker one for the high-income group, than "fundamental" rate changes (Table 12) which give rise to the same change of revenue.

This can be seen more conveniently from Table 16. There, the relative income effect for an increase in the exemption from $600 to $700 per capita is expressed as a ratio of the corresponding relative income effect resulting from an "across-the-board" rate reduction of the 1959 United States federal income tax by two percentage points. The steady decline of this ratio with increases in net income is quite conspicuous. Thus, for example, for a single person with no dependents, at the net income level of $1,000, the increase in the exemption of $100 results in a relative income effect two-and-a-half times as strong as that of the rate reduction of two percentage points (Table 16, column 2, line 1). At the net income level of $8,000, the increase in the exemption results in a relative income effect which is only one fifth of that due to the rate reduction (column 2, line 6). At the net income level of $500,000, the ratio is one to one hundred (column 2, line 12).

TABLE 16. *Relative income effect for an increase in the exemption from $600 to $700 per capita, expressed as a ratio of the corresponding relative income effect resulting from an "across-the-board" rate reduction of the 1959 United States federal income tax by 2 percentage points*

Net income (1)	relative income effect due to increase in exemption[a] / relative income effect due to rate reduction		
	Single person no dependents (2)	Married couple no dependents (3)	Married couple 2 dependents (4)
1,000	2.49	—	—
2,000	0.71	2.49	—
3,000	0.46	1.12	6.62
4,000	0.32	0.71	2.49
5,000	0.29	0.53	1.54
8,000	0.20	0.32	0.79
10,000	0.18	0.29	0.58
15,000	0.16	0.22	0.48
25,000	0.12	0.16	0.34
50,000	0.07	0.12	0.25
100,000	0.04	0.07	0.15
500,000	0.01	0.02	0.04

[a] The relative income effect is given by $\varepsilon(t/X)$. At any given net income level, the income elasticity of the demand for leisure (ε) is the same for both types of tax reduction. Hence the ratio of the two relative income effects is given by $t/X / t'/X'$, where the first fraction results from the increase in the exemption and the primed fraction results from the rate reduction.
Note:
Columns (2), (3), and (4) are computed by dividing columns (4), (7), and (10) of Table 12 into columns (4), (7), and (10) of Table 9 respectively.

A comparison of Tables 10 and 13 indicates that, given any set of price elasticities of the demand for leisure, adjustments of the size of the exemption (Table 10) will result in a stronger relative and absolute substitution effect for almost all taxpayers who experience a substitution effect than a "fundamental" rate adjustment which gives rise to the same change of revenue (Table 13). This can be seen more clearly from Table 17. There, the relative substitution effect for an

TABLE 17. *Relative substitution effect for an increase in the exemption from $600 to $700 per capita, expressed as a ratio of the corresponding relative substitution effect resulting from an "across-the-board" rate reduction of the 1959 United States federal income tax by 2 percentage points*

Net income range		relative substitution effect due to increase in exemption
Single person no dependents (1)	Married couple no dependents (2)	relative substitution effect due to rate reduction (3)
600–700	1,200–1,400	10.0
2,600–2,700	5,200–5,400	1.0
4,600–4,700	9,200–9,400	2.0
6,600–6,700	13,200–13,400	2.0
8,600–8,700	17,200–17,400	2.0
10,600–10,700	21,200–21,400	2.0
12,600–12,700	25,200–25,400	2.5
14,600–14,700	29,200–29,400	2.0
16,600–16,700	33,200–33,400	1.5
18,600–18,700	37,200–37,400	1.5
20,600–20,700	41,200–41,400	1.5
22,600–22,700	45,200–45,400	1.5
26,600–26,700	53,200–53,400	1.5
32,600–32,700	65,200–65,400	1.5
38,600–38,700	77,200–77,400	2.0
44,600–44,700	89,200–89,400	1.5
50,600–50,700	101,200–101,400	1.5
60,600–60,700	121,200–121,400	1.5
70,600–70,700	141,200–141,400	1.5
80,600–80,700	161,200–161,400	1.5
90,600–90,700	181,200–181,400	1.5
100,600–100,700	201,200–201,400	1.0
150,600–150,700	301,200–301,400	0.5
200,600–200,700	401,200–401,400	0.5

Note:
Column (3) is computed by dividing the "across-the-board" rate reduction of 2 per cent into the difference between adjacent marginal rates, as listed in column (6) of Table 10.

increase in the exemption from $600 to $700 per capita is expressed as a ratio of the corresponding relative substitution effect resulting from an "across-the-board" rate reduction of the United States federal income tax by two percentage points. It will be seen that, for most income levels, the increase in the exemption results in a relative substitution effect one-and-a-half to two times as strong as the one due to the rate reduction. This becomes obvious when we realize that the ratio between the two relative substitution effects is equivalent to the division of the difference between every pair of adjacent marginal rates by the "across-the-board" rate change.[46] Since the marginal rate schedule of the United States federal income tax progresses mostly by steps of three and four percentage points and the "across-the-board" rate reduction under consideration is two percentage points, the ratio of the substitution effects is 1.5–2.0 over most of the income range. However, at the lowest income level it is 10.0 and at the highest levels it is only 0.5.

One has to keep in mind that, in case of the increase in the exemption only about ten per cent of the taxpayers are affected by the substitution effect, whereas all taxpayers experience such an effect in case of the rate reduction. Of those taxpayers affected by the income effect and the substitution effect in both cases of revenue adjustment, the ones with medium and high incomes are likely to increase their amount of leisure demanded by a smaller proportion, or reduce it by a greater proportion, when the exemption is increased than when the rates are reduced. This can be readily seen by comparing Tables 16 and 17. The increase in the exemption results in a smaller relative and absolute income effect than the rate reduction for all but the lowest net income levels (that is, most figures in Table 16, columns (2), (3), and (4) are smaller than one), whereas it results in a greater relative and absolute substitution effect over all but the very highest relevant net income ranges (that is, all but the last two figures in Table 17, column (3) are greater than one).

What about those taxpayers who are affected by the substitution effect only in case of the rate reduction? Does the substitution effect

---

[46] The relative substitution effect is given by $\varepsilon_p[(r_n - r_{n-1})/(100 - r_n)]$ in case of the increase in the exemption (see Table 10) and by $\varepsilon_p[(-c)/(100 - r_n)]$ in case of the "across-the-board" rate change, where c represents the rate change (see Table 13). Thus, the ratio of the relative substitution effects is $(r_n - r_{n-1})/(-c)$.

compensate for the fact that their income effect is much greater than in case of an equal-revenue increase of the exemption over the major part of the net income range? Table 16 indicates that the rate reduction will result in a greater incentive-to-work effect than the increase in the exemption at low income levels. At low income levels, the rate reduction results in a smaller relative and absolute income effect than the increase in the exemption; moreover, this smaller income effect is opposed by the substitution effect. At medium and high income levels, the rate reduction results in a much greater relative and absolute income effect than the increase in the exemption, as can be seen from Table 16. Thus, in order for the rate reduction to provide a greater incentive-to-work effect at these income levels, at least a major part of its income effect would have to be offset by its substitution effect. The "equalizing ratios" of Table 14 indicate that such a major offsetting can be expected only if the income elasticity of the demand for leisure is either smaller, or not much greater, than the price elasticity of the demand for leisure.

In conclusion, our comparison of an increase in the per capita exemption of the 1959 United States federal income tax from $600 to $700 with an "across-the-board" rate reduction of two percentage points yields the following results: (1) Of those taxpayers affected by both the income effect and the substitution effect under both methods of tax reduction (about ten per cent of all taxable returns), the medium and upper income groups experience a stronger incentive-to-work effect in case of the increase of the exemption. At the low income level, the results are inconclusive.[47] (2) Of those taxpayers affected by both the income effect and the substitution effect only in case of the rate reduction,[48] the low-income group will experience a stronger incentive-to-work effect in case of the rate reduction. No definite conclusions can be reached with regard to the medium and upper income groups without the knowledge of at least the ratio between the income and price elasticity of the demand for leisure at those income levels.

---

[47] However, the low income level is of major importance, because the bulk of those ten per cent of all taxable returns are concentrated there (see Table 11).

[48] Those are the taxpayers who, in case of the increase in the exemption, are affected solely by the income effect.

Thus, only the fact that the low-income group mentioned under (2) is quite numerous lends some direct support to statements which maintain that a greater direct incentive-to-work effect can probably be obtained from rate reductions than from increases in the size of the exemption, assuming the same amount of revenue loss. Moreover, such statements are much too general and have little economic significance, since they are based, at best, upon the summation of non-homogeneous working hours of the entire labor force. Obviously, total hours worked may remain unchanged or increase, while total national product declines. From the point of view of national product, changes in hours worked should be weighted by the marginal revenue product which, in equilibirum, is equal to the marginal rate of remuneration.[49] The approach developed here, by relating changes in hours worked to the level of income, makes it *possible* to apply differential weights according to income level, (even though no attempt has been made here to apply such weights and to aggregate).[50] In this respect, our approach goes beyond the traditional analysis of incentives to work.[51]

E. Administrative Differences and Reversibility

For the sake of completeness, we shall briefly discuss the adminis-

---

[49] This implies that national product is measured in current terms, that is, changes in both quantity produced and product-price are taken into consideration. Under perfect competition, the marginal revenue product would be identical with the value of the marginal physical product and the weights applied would have additional significance from a welfare point of view.

[50] Empirically it is likely to be true that the weights applied should increase with the income level, even though it need not be so if a large part of the income is derived from property or if the dispersion of the number of hours worked (per day, week, year) around the average is substantial. Actually, the correlation between level of income and marginal (as well as average) rate of remuneration is likely to be very high.

[51] While revising the manuscript, I have encountered for the first time a brief explicit statement of the problem of wheighting and aggregating in Musgrave's new book *The Theory of Public Finance* (*op. cit.*, pp. 243–248). There MUSGRAVE points out that "the results that apply to the individual cannot be transferred mechanically to the group." In a footnote he states that "this aspect of the matter is usually overlooked" (*op. cit.*, p. 243).

trative differences and problems of reversibility arising out of statutory changes in revenue, though they are not of a purely analytical nature.

In countries which practice withholding at the source, the rate of withholding has to be adjusted for every statutory change in revenue, whether this be a change in the size of the exemption or a change of the rate schedule. If such adjustments have to be carried out in the middle of the income year, they are likely to increase substantially the number of cases with over-withholding or under-withholding, irrespective of the type of revenue adjustment that is selected.[52] In countries which do not practice withholding at the source, this problem does not arise. However, in all cases, the change in the "coverage" of taxpayers, due to a change in the size of the exemption, will create some additional difficulties. It is likely to increase or reduce greatly the number of active taxpayers, thereby making it more difficult to audit and process the returns or requiring changes in the staff of the internal revenue service of the country. However, these additional difficulties should not be overrated. Especially in countries like the United States, where income tax collection and social-security tax collection are coordinated, the additional administrative burden is likely to be extremely small.

Much more serious is the problem of reversibility of statutory revenue adjustments, that is, the problem of symmetrical changes in both upward and downward direction. As Professor VICKREY put it:

> A policy that consisted of systematically raising exemptions when the economy is to be stimulated, and of raising rates when inflation is to be restrained would of course soon result in a completely distorted tax structure, as would the reverse policy of lowering rates in recessions and lowering exemptions in booms.[53]

From a purely political point of view it seems doubtful, whether

---

[52] If the withholding rates are adjusted at that time (as they should be), the number of cases with over-withholding is likely to be increased somewhat more if the exemptions are increased than if the rates are reduced. (See VICKREY, *Adjustment of Income Tax Schedules for Small Incomes*, pp. 348–349).

[53] *Idem.*, p. 347.

exemptions can be changed frequently.[54] Such changes might be feasible only if they were completely separated from politics, that is, if they were automatic or quasi-automatic.[55] Thus, from the point of view of reversibility, rate changes are far more flexible and are better suited for frequent short-run adjustments, whereas changes in the exemptions may best be used for occasional adjustments of a more lasting and fundamental nature.[56]

---

[54] This is true for the U.S. income tax and similar systems. However, in cases like the British system, where changes in the size of exemptions or "allowances" are taken care of by "re-coding," this need not be true at all.

[55] E.g., the exemptions could be linked in some automatic way to the Consumer Price Index. On the basis of the "minimum-standard-of-living" argument, such a link would have to be cyclical, on the bases of the "fiscal-policy" argument, it would have to be counter-cyclical.

[56] Of course, the problem of reversibility arises with regard to rate changes, too. Spokesmen for the lower income groups are likely to favor equi-proportional rate increases and "across-the-board" rate reductions, whereas representatives of the upper income groups will tend to favor "across-the-board" rate increases and equi-proportional rate reductions. Adherence to any one of these schemes will result in a complete distortion of the tax after but a few rounds of rate increases and reductions.

CHAPTER V

QUASI-EXEMPTIONS UNDER PROGRESSIVE TAXATION

The analysis of income tax exemptions can hardly be considered complete, unless some attention is paid to the major types of "quasi-exemption." We use the term "quasi-exemption" for any supplement to, or substitute for, the genuine exemption. The major types of quasi-exemption are (1) the tax credit and (2) the "standard deduction."

A. The Tax Credit

The tax credit is defined as the reduction of the tentative tax liability either by a certain relative, or by a certain absolute, amount. The former case can be easily disposed of as being nothing more than a disguised reduction in the rate schedule. If the tax credit consists of a reduction of all tentative tax liabilities by a given proportion, this is equivalent to a reduction of the whole average-rate schedule by this proportion. We have proved previously,[1] that this can be achieved by reducing all marginal rates by that very same proportion. Thus, a tax credit of, say, five per cent would be nothing more than a disguised reduction of the whole marginal-rate schedule by five per cent. In principle, such an outright rate reduction is preferable to the round-about procedure of the tax credit, because it avoids the introduction of this additional concept and represents the simpler method of tax computation. However, in certain cases, the tax-credit method may be preferable, because of its greater flexibility. A tax credit can be voted and implemented even after all rate schedules and tax forms have been printed and sent to the

---

[1] See Chapter III, Section E, § 2 and *Mathematical Appendix* to Chapter III.

taxpayers. It is easy to compute refunds on tax payments which have already been received. Furthermore, this greater flexibility may cause the legislator to view the tax credit as a "temporary" measure, one that is more easily adopted than a new rate schedule. Thus, he may prefer the tax credit for "temporary" tax reductions.[2]

Up to now, we have assumed that the proportion of the tax credit is the same for all income groups and levels. However, the tax credit may be restricted to selective income groups, or the proportion of the tax credit may vary with the income level. In these cases, it may not always be possible to adjust a unique rate schedule in such a way as to achieve the same effect as that of the tax credit. A substitution of multiple rate schedules may be required to duplicate the effect of the single rate schedule plus tax credit. In this case, it is no longer true that such adjusted rate schedules are necessarily preferable, in principle. The tax-credit device may be simpler from the point of view of the taxpayer and the tax administrator.[3]

A completely different case is that of a tax credit representing a reduction of the tentative tax liability by a certain absolute amount. This is equivalent to an exemption which comes out of the first income bracket rather than out of the top bracket. The main difference between such a tax credit and an exemption is that in the former case the absolute value of the tax relief is constant throughout, whereas, in the latter case, it is constant within each tax bracket but increases from bracket to bracket.

The relative tax value of this type of tax credit declines in form of a single rectangular hyperbola with asymptotes $Y = 0$ and $V/Y = 0$.

---

[2] E.g., a tax credit may be enacted for a specific year. If it is not renewed thereafter, the tax is increased to its previous level without any active legislation. This devise has been used frequently by New York State.

The legislator may also shy away from tax rates which include decimal fractions of one per cent. For example, in case of the U.S. federal income tax, a rate reduction of five per cent would substitute the rates of 19%, 20.9%, 24.7%, etc. for 20%, 22%, 26%, etc. For the years 1946, 1947, such a tax credit of five per cent was effective in the United States. For complete tables of the equivalent effective marginal tax rates, see Prentice Hall, *Federal Tax Course 1948* (New York: Prentice Hall Inc., 1947), § 803–804.

[3] The U.S. income tax for the years 1948–50 furnishes a good example of the differential tax-credit device. For 1948 and 1949, the tax law states:

It will be noted that this pattern corresponds exactly to the relative tax value of the exemption under proportional taxation (see Chapter II, Section B). Thus, if the absolute (and relative) tax value of the tax credit is equal to that of the exemption, over the first income bracket, then it is smaller over all subsequent income brackets. Therefore, the average tax rate for all income brackets, except the first one, will be higher than it would be under the exemption. Correspondingly, more revenue will be collected and a compensating reduction of the tax rates is feasible.[4]

Over most of the income range, tax progressivity, as measured by the ARP, will be smaller with the tax credit than with a comparable exemption. However, over the ranges where the exemption shifts the net-income brackets, progressivity is likely to be increased by the tax credit.

The preceding analysis, though widely used, is of little consequence, because it is based on an inappropriate comparison. Two tax systems have been compared which differ with regard to their most important aspect: their revenue yield. The exemption system should be compared with a tax-credit system which yields exactly the same revenue. In case of a single-exemption system, such a comparison is easy. It can be shown that a single-exemption tax can

---

The combined normal tax and surtax under sec. 11 and subsection (b) of this section shall be the aggregate of the tentative normal tax and tentative surtax, reduced as follows:

If the aggregate is:	The reduction shall be:
Not over $400	17% of the aggregate.
Over $400 but not over $100,000	$68 plus 12% of excess over $400.
Over $100,000	$12,020 plus 9.75% of excess over $100,000.*

The corresponding reductions for 1950 were:

If the aggregate is:	The reduction shall be:
Not over $400	13% of the aggregate.
Over $400 but not over $100,000	$52 plus 9% of excess over $400.
Over $100,000	$9,016 plus 7.3% of excess over $100,000.*

* U.S. Internal Revenue Code 1939–1953 (Chicago, New York, Washington: Commerce Clearing House, Inc., 1954), sec. 12 (c).

[4] See Mathematical Appendix to Chapter v.

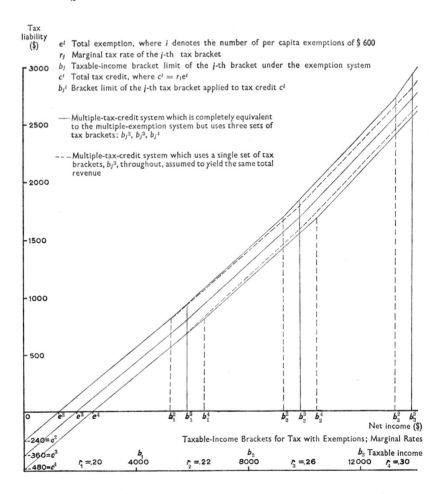

Tax liability ($)

e^i Total exemption, where i denotes the number of per capita exemptions of $600
r_j Marginal tax rate of the j-th tax bracket
b_j Taxable-income bracket limit of the j-th bracket under the exemption system
c^i Total tax credit, where $c^i = r_1 e^i$
b_j^i Bracket limit of the j-th tax bracket applied to tax credit c^i

—— Multiple-tax-credit system which is completely equivalent to the multiple-exemption system but uses three sets of tax brackets: b_j^2, b_j^3, b_j^4

– – – Multiple-tax-credit system which uses a single set of tax brackets, b_j^3, throughout, assumed to yield the same total revenue

Net income ($)

Taxable-Income Brackets for Tax with Exemptions; Marginal Rates

PLATE XI. Transformation of a multiple-exemption into a multiple-tax-credit system which yields the same total tax revenue
(1959 United States federal income tax for married couples without children, with one child, and with two children, assuming income splitting)

be expressed in form of an identical single-tax-credit tax. This is done in the following way: Let the tax credit be equal to the absolute tax value of the exemption within the first statutory bracket. Apply the same set of marginal tax rates as under the single-exemption plan, but increase the first taxable-income bracket, and each subsequent bracket limit, by an amount equal to the exemption. This new tax-credit system will yield the same average tax rates and ARP throughout, and will collect the same total revenue, as the exemption system. These "two systems" are but two different expressions for the same system.[5] However, the "exemption-system" is preferable, because it simplifies tax computations.

Most exemption systems are multiple-, rather than single-, exemption systems. The typical case is the one, found in many countries, where the exemption increases with the size of the family. In this case, no simple transformation into an equivalent multiple-tax-credit system is possible. The previous transformation could be applied to each exemption individually. However, in this case, a multiple-exemption system with a unique set of statutory tax rates and statutory (taxable-income) brackets would be expressed in the form of a multiple-tax-credit system with a unique set of statutory rates, but with several sets of statutory (taxable-income) brackets.[6] This is illustrated on Plate XI, a graphical presentation of the 1959 United States federal income tax for married couples without children, with one child, and with two children (assuming income splitting throughout). Under the present law, a unique set of marginal rates and of statutory (taxable-income) brackets is applied. If the exemptions (e^2, e^3, e^4) are replaced by the corresponding tax credits ($c^2 = r_1 e^2$, $c^3 = r_1 e^3$, $c^4 = r_1 e^4$), the new system will duplicate the exemption system, provided the previous set of statutory (taxable-income) brackets (b_1, b_2, b_3, . . .) is replaced by *three* new sets of brackets (b_1^2, b_2^2, b_3^2, . . .; b_1^3, b_2^3, b_3^3, . . .; b_1^4, b_2^4, b_3^4, . . .). The greater simplicity of the exemption system is obvious.

However, as a rule, tax-credit systems employ but a single set of

---

[5] For mathematical proofs, see *Mathematical Appendix* to Chapter v. It is, of course, implied that the effective tax liability shall not fall below zero.

[6] For mathematical proofs, see *Mathematical Appendix* to Chapter v.

statutory rates and tax brackets. In this case, the basis for comparison should be a multiple-tax-credit system which collects the same total revenue as the multiple-exemption system and employs but a single set of statutory rates and tax brackets. Such a system can be found. But, while collecting the same total revenue as the exemption system, it will collect less revenue from the smallest families, and more revenue from the largest families.[7] This is due to the fact that the tax differential between families of different size increases with their income, when a multiple-exemption system is used, while it remains constant, when a multiple-tax-credit system is applied.

This redistribution of the tax burden according to the size of the family is illustrated on Plate XI (broken lines). There it is assumed (for the purpose of illustration) that total tax revenue is the same as with the multiple-exemption system, if the multiple-tax-credit system uses the unique set of tax brackets $b_1^3, b_2^3, b_3^3, \ldots$ throughout.

In conclusion, we have shown that a multiple-exemption system of allowances for size of family (in contrast to a multiple-tax-credit system) accords with the assumption that each additional dependent "costs" more, in a higher-income family, than in a lower-income one. Furthermore, a transformation of a multiple-exemption system into a multiple-tax-credit system will increase the tax burden of large families, and reduce the tax burden of small families, especially in the upper income ranges.

B. The Standard Deduction

We shall use the term "standard deduction" for a quasi-exemption that is expressed as a percentage of some income concept. The term is taken from the United States federal income tax, which provides a standard deduction of ten per cent of "adjusted gross income," but not exceeding 1,000 dollars.[8] In the United States, the standard deduction is used as a simplifying alternative, at the taxpayer's

---

[7] See *Mathematical Appendix* to Chapter v.

[8] *U.S. Internal Revenue Code, 1954 Code Edition*, sec. 141. However "in case of a separate return by a married individual the standard deduction shall not exceed $500" *(ibid.)*.

option, to the "itemized deductions" of legally deductible non-business expenditures. Its proponents may argue that the itemized deductions have a tendency to increase with increases in income and that the simplifying alternative should preserve this feature. However, not all non-business deductions show a consistent positive correlation with income. Furthermore, better solutions to the problem are feasible.[9]

At present, it is not our task to pass judgment on the standard deduction, but rather to analyze its impact on the tax structure. Such an analysis may, of course, provide the foundation for subsequent evaluation. We shall follow the same sequence that was used in the analysis of the exemption. First, we shall determine the absolute and relative tax value of the standard deduction, thereafter—the impact on the average tax rate and the ARP. We shall assume throughout that the standard deduction is superimposed on the exemption (which, as a limiting case, may be zero).[10] For the convenience of our analysis, we shall distinguish between two types of income ranges: Type I, where taxable income prior to the deduction of the standard deduction falls within a higher taxable-income bracket than after the deduction, and Type II, where taxable income falls within the same taxable-income bracket before and after the deduction of the standard deduction.[11]

1. THE ABSOLUTE TAX VALUE OF THE STANDARD DEDUCTION

The absolute tax value of the standard deduction increases throughout as income increases. This increase is linear over each range of both Type I and Type II, but the rates of increase differ. Over each range of Type II, the absolute tax value of the standard

---

[9] E.g., see WILLIAM VICKREY, *Agenda for Progressive Taxation* (New York: The Ronald Press Co., 1947), p. 371.

[10] Our treatment implies a comparison of the standard deduction with the alternative of "no deduction." Actually, in absence of the standard deduction, even those who use it at present would itemize their deductions. However, itemized deduction vary from person to person and provide no solid basis for comparison.

[11] For a similar division, see Chapter III, Sections A and B.

deduction increases at a rate equal to the product of the rate of the standard deduction times the highest marginal rate which would be effective in the absence of the standard deduction (that is, sr_n).[12] Since the marginal rate increases from bracket to bracket, the absolute tax value of the standard deduction will increase (linearly) at a faster and faster rate from bracket to bracket. Over each range of Type I, the absolute tax value of the standard deduction also increases linearly, but at a faster rate than over either the preceeding or the following range of Type II.[13]

This pattern of the absolute tax value of the standard deduction is shown in Plate XII which presents the absolute tax value of the standard deduction and of the exemption for single persons with no dependents, according to the 1959 United States federal income tax.

2. THE RELATIVE TAX VALUE OF THE STANDARD DEDUCTION

For the ranges of Type II, the relative tax value of the standard deduction remains constant within each bracket and is equal to the product of the rate of the standard deduction times the highest marginal rate which would be effective in absence of the standard deduction (i.e., sr_n). Since the marginal rate increases from bracket to bracket, so does the relative tax value of the standard deduction. This increase is achieved by an increase of the relative tax value of the standard deduction over each range of Type I.[14]

3. THE IMPACT OF THE STANDARD DEDUCTION ON THE AVERAGE TAX RATE AND THE AVERAGE-RATE PROGRESSION (ARP)

It has been shown that, by definition, the impact on the average tax rate is given by the deduction of the relative tax value from the

---

[12] For a more explicit mathematical treatment, see *Mathematical Appendix* to Chapter v.

[13] The expression of this rate of increase is somewhat more complicated. It is $sr_{n+1} + r_{n+1} - r_n$ (see *Mathematical Appendix* to Chapter v).

[14] For a more explicit mathematical treatment, see *Mathematical Appendix* to Chapter v.

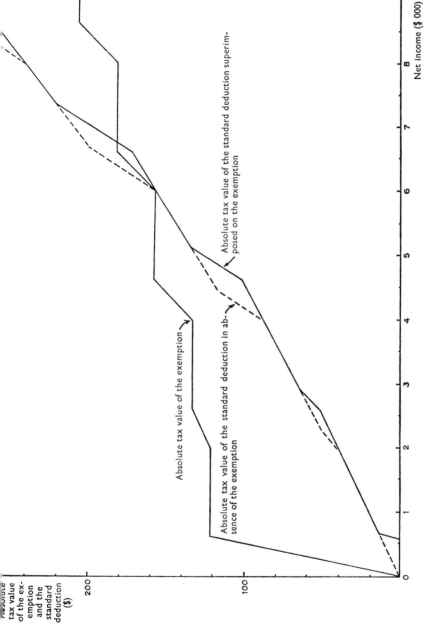

PLATE XII. Absolute tax value of the exemption and of the standard deduction for single persons with no dependents according to the 1959 United States federal income tax "would-be" average tax rate. Thus, deducting the relative tax value of the standard deduction, we get the following results. Within each range of Type II, the average rate is reduced by a constant amount which increases from bracket to bracket. This increase is achieved by the increase of the relative tax value of the standard deduction over the transition-ranges of Type I. Apropos, it is interesting to notice that the increases of the relative tax value of the standard deduction over the ranges of Type I is equivalent to shifting the net-income brackets over these ranges, i.e., shifting them by an amount of $s/(1-s)(Y_{n-1})$.[15] A similar effect had been noted previously with regard to the transition-ranges of the exemption.[16] These shifts in the net-income brackets are illustrated in Table 18.

TABLE 18. *Shifts in the net-income brackets (i.e., in the effective starting points of the marginal rates) due to the exemption and the standard deduction, as illustrated by the 1959 United States federal income tax for single persons with no dependents*

Marginal tax rate	Taxable-income bracket limit	Shift due to exemption of $600	Shift due to standard deduction of 10%	Effective net-income bracket limit[a]
(%)	($)	($)	($)	($)
(1)	(2)	(3)	(4)	(5)
20	0	600	67	667
22	2,000	600	289	2,889
26	4,000	600	511	5,111
30	6,000	600	733	7,333
34	8,000	600	956	9,556
38	10,000	600	1,000[b]	11,600

Notes:

[a] Net income—in this case "adjusted gross income." See *U.S. Internal Revenue Code, 1954 Code Edition*, secs. 62 and 141.

[b] The U.S. standard deduction is limited to a maximum of $1,000. (See *U.S. Internal Revenue Code, 1954 Code Edition*, sec. 141.) Thus for incomes of $10,000 and over, the standard deduction, if used at all, amounts in effect to an increase in the exemption by $1,000, and the analysis for changes in the size of the exemption has to be applied (in case of a separate return by a married individual, the limit is $500. *Ibid.*).

[15] See *Mathematical Appendix* to Chapter v.
[16] See Chapter III, Section C.

Over the ranges of Type II, the ARP is not affected at all by the standard deduction. Over the ranges of Type I, the ARP is somewhat reduced. Thus, the general pattern and level of the ARP is fairly well preserved. Only in the neighborhood of the discontinuities, a slower increase and tapering off replaces the vertical jump.

MATHEMATICAL
APPENDICES

MATHEMATICAL APPENDIX TO CHAPTER I

The tax liability R of an individual whose net income is Y, is computed according to most taxation plans in three steps.

First, an amount $e(Y)$ called the "exemption" is deducted from Y, the resulting difference $g(Y) = Y - e(Y)$ being the "taxable income." Then, the tax on any differential dg of taxable income is obtained by multiplying dg by the "statutory marginal rate" $r(g)$. Finally, the total tax liability is computed by integrating over the extent of the taxable income. Joining the three steps into one, we have

$$R = f(Y) = \int_0^{Y-e(Y)} r(g)dg.$$

The function $r(g)$ is in many cases a step-function taking on a finite number of values r_i. In that case the integral reduces to a finite sum.

The function $e(Y)$ is usually restricted to one of four forms. All four have in common the existence of an initial interval, say from 0 to $\bar{e}$, in which $Y = e(Y)$ holds. For values of Y beyond $\bar{e}$, we have one of the following possibilities:
(1) For $Y \geq \bar{e}$ $e(Y) = 0$ identically ("initial exemption").
(2) For $Y \geq \bar{e}$ $e(Y) = \bar{e}$ identically ("continuing exemption").
(3) For $Y \geq \bar{e}$ $e(Y)$ declines to zero in form of a decreasing step-function.
(4) For $Y \geq \bar{e}$ $e(Y)$ declines to zero linearly with constant slope k, and remains 0 afterwards.

Pigou imposed the following conditions on $f(Y)$:
1. $f(o) = 0$.
2. $f(Y)$ is non-decreasing.

127

3. $f(Y)/Y$ is monotone.

4. $f(Y) \leq Y$.

According to Pigou those conditions should imply convexity of $f(Y)$, which is not the case, as can be seen by the example $f(Y) = Y^2(2 - Y)$ for $0 \leq Y \leq 1$. As we have $f'(Y) = Y(4 - 3Y)$ and $(f(Y)/Y)' = 2 - 2Y$, Pigou's conditions hold, yet the second derivative $f''(Y) = 4 - 6Y$ changes sign at $Y = 2/3$, proving that f is not convex.

On the other hand, convexity implies Pigou's third condition, if the two first conditions are assumed. This follows from the fact that condition 3. is equivalent to the statement: "any segment joining the origin with a point on the tax curve lies entirely above the curve;" while convexity is equivalent to the stronger statement: "any segment joining two points on the curve lies entirely above the curve." A reasonable requirement that does not follow from any of the conditions mentioned, is the requirement that the income left after taxation should be an increasing function of the net income. Adding to this requirement the convexity condition, and the existence of an initial tax-free interval, we can state the three tax criteria. I. For an interval $0 \leq Y \leq \bar{e}$, $f(Y) = 0$. II. $f(Y)$ is convex. III. $Y - f(Y)$ is increasing. $f(Y)$ is in general not required to be differentiable. When the derivative exists, it is referred to as the "effective marginal rate." In that case, the third condition is equivalent to condition III'. $f'(Y) < 1$.

As convexity implies continuity, tax criterion II rules out the discontinuous exemption functions, namely types (1) ("initial exemption") and (3) ("decreasing step-function"). Considering the linearly declining exemption—which includes the continuing exemption as a special case with $k = 0$—we can compute $f'(Y)$ from the defining formula: $f'(Y) = r(g(Y)) \cdot (Y - e(Y))'$, where $g(Y)$ denotes the "taxable income" $Y - e(Y)$. The second factor equals $1 + k$ in the range of decline; therefore, the third tax criterion requires $(1 + k) r(Y - e(Y)) < 1$ throughout that range. In particular, considering the endpoint of that range, $Y = \bar{e}(1 + 1/k)$, we have $(1 + k) r(\bar{e}(1 + 1/k)) < 1$. For values of Y beyond the range of decline, $e(Y) = 0$ and the condition becomes simply $r(Y) < 1$. Now, considering tax criterion II, we can assure convexity by having $f'(Y)$

increase throughout. Except at the endpoint of the range of decline, this amounts to having $r(g)$ increase. At that point, $Y = \bar{e}(1 + 1/k)$, however, $r(g)$ has to jump in order to bridge the gap between the two formulae for $f'(Y)$, to the left and to the right of that point. Denoting by r^- and r^+ the limits of $r(g)$ as g tends to $\bar{e}(1 + 1/k)$ from the left and the right resp., the required jump is described by $r^+ \geq (1 + k)r^-$.

If $r(g)$ has the required jump, is a non-decreasing function, and is always less than unity, all three tax criteria will be met.

A taxation plan with linearly declining exemption is fully determined by the function $r(g)$, and by the numbers k and $\bar{e}$. The problem of finding a different plan, with continuing exemption, that will result in the same tax function $f(Y)$, has a unique solution. The number $\bar{e}$, being the maximal tax-free income, will remain the same in the new plan. $r(g)$ will change. Denoting the new statutory marginal rate by $q(g)$, we get for all $Y > \bar{e}$ $f'(Y) = q(Y - \bar{e})$. This has to equal the previous expression for $f'(Y)$, namely, $(1 + k)r(g_1(Y))$ in the decline-range, and $r(g_1(Y))$ beyond that range. $g_1(Y)$ denotes here the taxable income in the original plan, which equals $(1 + k) \times (Y - \bar{e})$ in the decline-range, and co-incides with Y for larger Y. Equating the original $f'(Y)$ with $q(Y - \bar{e})$, we arrive at the following definition of the function $q(g)$:

For $0 \leqslant g < \bar{e}/k$ $q(g) = (1 + k)r((1 + k)g)$.

For $\bar{e}/k \leqslant g$ $q(g) = r(g + \bar{e})$.

For the transformed version of the taxation plan, the conditions will all be fulfilled if and only if $q(g)$ is non-decreasing and less than 1. In the cases other than continuing exemption, we have seen that increasing $r(g)$ is not sufficient to imply condition II. The assumption of increasing $r(g)$ is therefore referred to as the "weaker form of condition II."

The class of taxation plans treated in Chapter II is characterized by the statutory marginal rate $r(g)$ being a constant throughout. The exemptions considered are of the linearly declining and the continuing types. Any plan in this class is completely determined by three constants: the maximum exemption $\bar{e}$, the rate of decline k, and the constant statutory marginal rate $\bar{r}$. As we can now take the constant $\bar{r}$ out of the integral in the defining formula of $f(Y)$, we simply have

$$R = f(Y) = [Y - e(Y)]\bar{r}.$$

Substituting the values for $e(Y)$, we get

For	$0 \leqslant Y < \bar{e}$	$f(Y) = 0.$
For	$\bar{e} \leqslant Y < \bar{e} + \bar{e}/k$	$f(Y) = (Y - \bar{e})(k + 1)\bar{r}.$
For	$\bar{e} + \bar{e}/k \leqslant Y$	$f(Y) = \bar{r}Y.$

Would there have been no exemption, we would have $f(Y) = \bar{r}Y$ throughout. Therefore, subtracting from $\bar{r}Y$ the actual tax liability, we find the absolute tax value of the exemption $V(Y)$:

For	$0 \leqslant Y < \bar{e}$	$V(Y) = \bar{r}Y.$
For	$\bar{e} \leqslant Y < \bar{e} + \bar{e}/k$	$V(Y) = \bar{r}[(k + 1)\bar{e} - kY].$
For all other Y		$V(Y) = 0.$

Next, we can compute the quantity mentioned by Pigou in his third condition, the "average tax rate" $f(Y)/Y$. We find its value to be 0 for Y smaller than $\bar{e}$, $\bar{r}(k + 1)(1 - \bar{e}/Y)$ within the decline-range, and $\bar{r}$ for larger Y. The average-rate progression, $[d/dY][f(Y)/Y]$, will be different from zero only within the decline-range, where it will equal $\bar{r}(k + 1)\bar{e}/Y^2$. Its maximum is therefore achieved at an income level equal to the maximum exemption, and equals $\bar{r}(k + 1)/\bar{e}$.

By subtracting the actual average tax rate from the rate which would prevail in a tax plan with the same $\bar{r}$ but without exemption, we get V/Y, the relative tax value of the exemption. From the various formulae developed in this section, one can see how the average-rate progression and the absolute and relative tax values depend on the different parameters. The influence of particular changes in the parameters is traced in Chapter II.

In Chapter III the statutory marginal rate is not assumed to be constant anymore. Instead, we assume that $r(g)$ is an increasing step-function. However, only the case of a continuing exemption is treated here.

Our taxation plan is now completely determined by the maximum exemption $\bar{e}$, by the points g_1, g_2, ... at which $r(g)$ changes value, and by the values r_1, r_2, ... that $r(g)$ achieves in the adjacent intervals $(0, g_1)$, (g_1, g_2), ... respectively.

The integral that expresses $f(Y)$, being the integral of a step-function, reduces now to a sum. Each term in this sum is the constant r_i multiplied by the corresponding interval of integration. In the case of a continuing exemption the upper limit of the integral has the value zero for $Y \leq \bar{e}$, and $Y - \bar{e}$ for larger Y; therefore the endpoint of the last interval in the integral is $Y - \bar{e}$. The other intervals have the points g_i as their endpoints, for all $g_i < Y - \bar{e}$. Therefore we have:

$$f(Y) = g_1 r_1 + (g_2 - g_1)r_2 + \ldots + (g_{n-1} - g_{n-2})r_{n-1} + (Y - \bar{e} - g_{n-1})r_n,$$

where g_{n-1} is the largest g_i still less than $Y - \bar{e}$.

$f(Y)$ is now a continuous, increasing, piecewise linear function.

The intervals in which it is linear have the points $Y_i = g_i + \bar{e}$ as endpoints. The "net-income brackets" (Y_i, Y_{i+1}) are thus simply a translation to the right by $\bar{e}$ of the "taxable-income brackets" (g_i, g_{i+1}). The tax liability $f(Y)$ can be expressed directly in terms of the net income brackets:

$$f(Y) = (Y_1 - \bar{e})r_1 + (Y_2 - Y_1)r_2 + \ldots + (Y - Y_{n-1})r_n,$$

but one must keep in mind that the numbers Y_i, for a fixed function $r(g)$, do depend on the maximum exemption $\bar{e}$.

There is still a third way of describing $f(Y)$ in this case. In each bracket, the function describes a straight line. In general, any straight line with positive Y-intercept and positive slope $\bar{r}$, can be regarded as resulting from a taxation plan with a continuing exemption and a constant statutory marginal rate. The maximum exemption in that plan will equal to the Y-intercept, and the marginal rate to $\bar{r}$. Considering the straight line that describes our given plan throughout the n-th income bracket, we can now ask for the plan with a constant $r(g)$ that would yield that same line. The given line, having slope r_n and passing through the point $(Y_n, f(Y_n))$, is given by

$$R = f(Y_n) + (Y - Y_n)r_n.$$

By setting R equal to zero, we find the Y-intercept:

$$Y = Y_n - f(Y_n)/r_n.$$

We see that a taxation plan with continuing exemption and constant marginal rate will agree with the given plan in its n-th bracket if we choose for the constant rate the number r_n, and for the maximum exemption the value $Y_n - f(Y_n)/r_n$, which is called "bracket exemption" and denoted by e_n. Once the numbers e_n are known, $f(Y)$ can be computed by finding the bracket into which Y falls, and using the formula:

$$f(Y) = (Y - e_n)r_n.$$

For computing the bracket exemption we could also have used the lower endpoint of the bracket, which leads to $e_n = Y_{n-1} - f(Y_{n-1})/r_n$. By combining this with the expression for e_{n-1} from the other formula, which is $e_{n-1} = Y_{n-1} - f(Y_{n-1})/r_{n-1}$, we can eliminate $f(Y_{n-1})$ and get a recursion formula:

$$e_n = Y_{n-1} - (Y_{n-1} - e_{n-1})r_{n-1}/r_n.*$$

As the numbers $f(Y_n)$ are usually available in the tax tables, the

---

* FOLLIET (*op. cit.*, pp. 100–101) also derived this recursion formula.

first formula for e_n is more convenient for computation than the recursion formula.

The tax value of the exemption in the type of plan considered here, is most easily found when the first form of $f(Y)$ is used. The number $\bar{e}$ appears explicitly only in the last summand. However, as g_{n-1} is the largest g_i still less than $Y - \bar{e}$, changing $\bar{e}$ to zero may result in changing the index n: it may shift Y into another income bracket. If $\bar{e}$ does not exceed $Y_n - Y$, this will not happen, and the elimination of the exemption will increase the tax liability by $r_n \cdot \bar{e}$. If $\bar{e} > Y_n - Y$, abolishing the exemption will shift Y into a higher bracket, whose index is the first i for which $\bar{e} < Y_n - Y$. If $\bar{e}$ is assumed to be smaller than all the differences $Y_i - Y_{i-1}$, Y can shift at most one bracket up. In that case, that part of $\bar{e}$ that "fills up" the taxable-income bracket, i.e. $Y_n - Y$, will add to $f(Y)$ the amount $(Y_n - Y)r_n$. The rest of $\bar{e}$, which is $\bar{e} - (Y_n - Y)$, will add another $(\bar{e} - (Y_n - Y))r_{n+1}$. We can therefore write:

For $Y_{n-1} < Y < Y_n - \bar{e}$ $V(Y) = \bar{e}r_n,$

for $Y_n - \bar{e} < Y < Y_n$ $V(Y) = Y_n r_n + (\bar{e} - Y_n)r_{n+1} + (r_{n+1} - r_n)Y.$

As $f(Y)$ is continuous and convex, and $V(Y) = f(Y + \bar{e}) - f(Y)$, $V(Y)$ is non decreasing, and also continuous. The behaviour of the relative tax value $V(Y)/Y$ can be seen directly from the formula for $V(Y)$: its graph is made up of continuously joining pieces of hyperbolas, two in each income bracket, the first always decreasing, the second increasing or decreasing, depending on the sign of $d(V/Y)/dY$, hence depending on whether $(Y_n - \bar{e})r_{n+1} - Y_n r_n \gtreqless 0$. Since $Y_n = g_n + \bar{e}$, this condition is equivalent to $(r_{n+1} - r_n)g_n - \bar{e}r_n \gtreqless 0$. This latter condition has been used in Chapter III; it has the added convenience that g_n is usually given by the tax laws and that it does not change with changes in the size of the exemption, as is the case with Y_n.

The average tax rate can be expressed in our case as a weighted average of the numbers $0, r_1, r_2, \ldots, r_n$, the first with weight $\bar{e}$, the last with weight $Y - Y_{n-1}$, the others weighted with the lengths of the corresponding income brackets. The sequence r_i increases, and, with growing Y, we keep adding weight at the right; therefore the average rate also will increase in accordance with the general considerations in Chapter I. As in the case of the relative tax value, the graph of the average rate consists of continuously joining arcs of hyperbolas. The average-rate progression, being the derivative of the average rate, can be found by using the third form of $f(Y)$, the bracket-exemption form: $f(Y) = (Y - e_n)r_n$.

We get:

$$f(Y)/Y = (1 - e_n/Y)r_n,$$

$$\frac{d}{dY}\left(f(Y)/Y\right) = e_n r_n/Y^2.$$

We can now use the formulae developed in this section, and study the impact of various changes in the statutory marginal rates r_i on the quantities we have computed. In keeping with the tax criteria, only those changes are admissible which leave the sequence r_i increasing, and its elements less than one.

The simplest possible change is a proportional change of all r_i. The quantities $f(Y)$, $f(Y)/Y$ and their Y-derivatives are all linear homogeneous in the r_i, and therefore they will change by an equal proportion. The bracket exemptions are homogeneous of degree zero in the r_i, and are therefore invariant under a proportional change of the latter. Geometrically, this follows from the fact that the Y-intercepts of a family of lines will not change if the R–Y-plane is transformed in the R-direction only.

A more general class of changes is obtained by multiplying the sequence r_i by a monotone sequence of numbers all greater than one. This class can also be characterized by stating that all r_i increase, while the quotients r_i/r_{i-1} either all increase, or all decrease. As a result of a change of this type, $f(Y)$ and $f(Y)/Y$ will be increased. So will $f'(Y)$, as the values it takes on are the numbers r_i. The average-rate progression, however, is proportional to the products $e_i r_i$, and its behavior depends on that of the bracket exemptions. In the recursion formula, the bracket exemption appears as an increasing function of the preceding bracket exemption, and of the ratio r_i/r_{i-1}. We have assumed that all these ratios change in the same direction; hence all bracket exemptions will change in that same direction too. If they increase, the numbers $e_i r_i$ have both their factors increase, and so will the average-rate progression $e_i r_i / Y^2$. If they decrease, we can make no general statement about the impact on the average-rate progression.

The class of changes with increasing r_i and decreasing r_i/r_{i-1} includes the important case of adding a constant to all r_i ("across-the-board"). As this type of change leaves the differences $r_i - r_{i-1}$ invariant, a connexion between the differences $r_i - r_{i-1}$ and the average-rate progression would be useful. In order to obtain such a connexion, we can multiply the recursion formula for e_i by r_i. We get a recursion formula for the numbers $e_n r_n$:

$$e_n r_n = e_{n-1} r_{n-1} + (r_n - r_{n-1}) Y_{n-1}.$$

We see from this formula that the difference between consecutive $e_n r_n$ remains unchanged by an "across-the-board" change, and that the $e_i r_i$ will all change by the same amount as the first one, $\bar{e} r_1$. In a change that increases all the differences, the $e_i r_i$ will all increase. If some or all of the differences $r_i - r_{i-1}$ decrease, we can again make no general statement, except about the first bracket. Even if just one difference decreases, all numbers $e_i r_i$ from that index on may decrease if Y_{n-1} is sufficiently large.

We can sum up by stating: An increase in the marginal rates will certainly cause an increase in the average-rate progression if one of the following conditions holds: 1. None of the ratios r_i/r_{i-1} is decreased. 2. None of the differences $r_i - r_{i-1}$ is decreased.

Let us assume that the maximum exemption of a taxation plan is increased by a quantity $\triangle\bar{e}$. The tax liability will decrease from $f(Y)$ to $f(Y - \triangle\bar{e})$, and the difference $\triangle X$ will appear as the increase in the disposable income $Y - f(Y)$. This increase is closely related to the absolute tax value of the exemption. The latter, being equal to $f(Y + \bar{e}) - f(Y)$, has been computed in the previous chapter without using the role of the number $\bar{e}$ in the taxation plan. We may therefore use the formulae for $V(Y)$ to compute the quantity $f(Y) - f(Y - \triangle\bar{e})$, by making the following changes:

1. replacing $\bar{e}$ by $-\triangle\bar{e}$, 2. changing the sign of the whole expression, and 3. replacing the shift into a higher bracket by a shift into a lower one. This way we get the result

For $\quad Y_{n-1} \leqslant Y < Y_{n-1} + \triangle\bar{e}$
$$f(Y) - f(Y - \triangle\bar{e}) = -Y_n r_n + (\triangle\bar{e} + Y_n)r_{n-1} + (r_n - r_{n-1})Y.$$

For $\quad Y_{n-1} + \triangle\bar{e} < Y \leqslant Y_n \quad f(Y) - f(Y - \triangle\bar{e}) = \triangle\bar{e}r_n.$

Just like $V(Y)$, $\triangle X$ is alternating between intervals of constancy to intervals of linear increase. Its derivative is correspondingly zero and $(r_n - r_{n-1})$. The "percentage increase of disposable income," $\triangle X/(Y - f(Y))$ will be, like the relative tax value, described by arcs of hyperbolas, two in each income bracket.

In the first part of each bracket, the function is of the form $(aY + b)/(cY + d)$, and the sign of its derivative will be the same as of the determinant $ad-bc$, which equals in this case $(r_n - r_{n-1})e_n r_n - (1 - r_n)[-Y_n r_n + (\triangle\bar{e} + Y_n)r_{n-1}]$ or after some arranging $(r_n - r_{n-1})[e_n r_n + Y_n(1 - r_n)] - (1 - r_n)\triangle\bar{e}r_{n-1}$. This expression may be positive in some brackets, negative in others; $\triangle X/X$ will increase or decrease accordingly.

In the second part of the bracket $\triangle X/X$ always decreases.

Apart from the question of the local decline of $\triangle X/X$, we can compare its values at the bracket boundaries. Using the formula for the second part of a bracket, we find that at $Y = Y_n$

$$\frac{\triangle X}{X} = \frac{\triangle \bar{e} r_n}{Y_n - f(Y_n)}.$$

This will be less than the corresponding value at $Y = Y_{n-1}$ if and only if the inequality

$$\frac{Y_n - f(Y_n)}{Y_n - Y_{n-1}} < \frac{r_n(1 - r_n)}{r_n - r_{n-1}}$$

holds. A simple special case is obtained when the bracket width $Y_n - Y_{n-1}$ is the same B for all n. In that case $f(Y_n)$ becomes $B \cdot \sum\limits_{i=1}^{n} r_i$, Y_n becomes $\bar{e} + nB$ and the inequality reduces to

$$\bar{e}/B < \frac{(1 - r_n)r_n}{r_n - r_{n-1}} - \sum_{i=1}^{n}(1 - r_i).$$

From the above expressions it is evident that the sign of $[(\triangle X/X) \text{ at } Y_n] - [(\triangle X/X) \text{ at } Y_{n-1}]$ depends on the particular tax structure. Any one of the following measures will increase $[(\triangle X/X) \text{ at } Y_n]$ relative to $[(\triangle X/X) \text{ at } Y_{n-1}]$. (1) An increase in the tax bracket $(Y_n - Y_{n-1})$, (2) a reduction in the rate increment $(r_n - r_{n-1})$, (3) a change of r_n towards $r_n = 0.5$ (which is the maximum value for the numerator $r_n(1 - r_n)$.

In this chapter we consider some taxation plans that involve new parameters.

The first class of plans to be considered is defined by a sequence of income brackets with a corresponding sequence of marginal rates, and a positive constant c, called "tax credit." The tax liability in this class is computed by integrating the marginal rate over the entire net income, and subtracting the constant c from the result. Whenever this procedure results in a negative number, the liability is assumed to be zero.

Clearly, the class of all functions $f(Y)$ obtained in this way is the class of all increasing, convex, piecewise linear functions with slopes less than one, and a positive Y-intercept. We should therefore be able to transform any taxation plan with a continuing exemption into one of the new type. This can indeed be done, and the necessary parameters are determined by the following considerations:

1. The numbers $\bar{e}$ and c are the Y- and f-intercepts, respectively, of the line corresponding to the first bracket, and the slope of that line is r_1; hence, we must have $c = r_1\bar{e}$.

2. The numbers r_i represent the slopes in the various brackets and must be the same in the new plan. Since the bracket limits g_i, however, determine the points of changing slope in the new plan, they must coincide with the *net*-income bracket-limits of the original plan.

In some cases it may be impractical to carry out the change in the taxable-income brackets required by the transformation, and, while the value $r_1\bar{e}$ is again used for the tax credit, the numbers g_i are left unchanged. The function $f(Y)$ obtained this way will differ from the original $f(Y)$. By first abolishing the exemption and then

introducing the tax credit, the graph of f(Y) is translated first to
the left by $\bar{e}$ and then downward by c. The line corresponding to
the first bracket will return by the second translation to its original
position, and the rest of the graph will lie above the graph of the
original f(Y).

The tax liability has therefore been increased for all $Y > g_1$. The
average rate f(Y)/Y has been increased too. The average-rate progression, for which we found the expression $e_n r_n / Y^2$, can also be
described as the ratio between the absolute value of the f-intercept
and the squared net income. By our transformation all lines from
the second bracket on move up, and their f-intercepts decrease in
absolute value; therefore for those values of Y which are not shifted
into a higher bracket in the new plan, the average-rate progression
has been decreased. For the other values of Y, the result is not as
clear; the comparison shows that in the n-th bracket the average-rate
progression for values of Y that are shifted into a higher bracket is
decreased if and only if

$$ r_{n+1} < r_n + (r_n - r_1)\bar{e}/g_n. $$

For $n = 1$ this condition can never be fulfilled. For $n > 1$ it
requires a very slowly increasing sequence r_i. In practice, the
condition is not likely to hold for any n.

The problem of transforming a taxation plan with a continuing
exemption into one with tax credits becomes more involved when
the maximum exemption is not the same for all individuals, but
depends on some variable j. The tax liability becomes in that case
a function f(Y, j) of two variables. In order to transform this plan
into a plan with tax credits depending on j, we have to choose
$c^j = r_1 e^j$, and $g_i^j = g_i + e^j$. We would now have a different set of
income brackets for each value of j. If we introduce the required
tax credits, but retain the original taxable-income brackets g_i, the
function f(Y, j) will change. In particular, its values for all brackets
beyond the first will increase. This way the dependence of the
bracket structure on j is avoided. If in addition to having brackets
that do not depend on j, we wish to keep unchanged the total
revenue collected from the population, we can choose as bracket
limits $g_i^* = g_i + e^*$, where e^*, a value between the highest and the

lowest e^j, can be found if the joint distribution of Y and j in the population is known. For values j with $e^j > e^*$ the plan using e^* has a higher $f(Y, j)$ than the original plan; for $e^j < e^*$ it has a lower $f(Y, j)$.

A further class of taxation plans consists of the plans in which in addition to the exemption, an amount proportional to net income is deducted before the marginal rates are applied. This amount sY is called the "standard deduction." Its tax value can be found by a similar computation to that of the tax value of an exemption. Whenever there would be no shift of bracket when the deduction is abolished, its tax value is sYr_n. If a shift occurs, $Y_n - Y$ contributes an increase of $(Y_n - Y)r_n$ to the tax liability, and the rest of sY, contributes $(sY - (Y_n - Y))r_{n+1}$. The absolute tax value is in this case

$$[(1 + s)r_{n+1} - r_n]Y - (r_{n+1} - r_n)Y_n.$$

Clearly the absolute tax value increases throughout, while the relative tax value is alternatingly constant and increasing. Its derivative, that equals to the change in the average-rate progression due to abolishing the standard deduction, is thus alternatingly zero and positive.

Geometrically, introducing the standard deduction is equivalent to stretching the graph of $f(Y)$ in the Y-direction by a factor of $1/(1 - s)$; the net-income bracket-limits will shift to the right accordingly.

LIST OF BASIC NOTATIONS

c – Tax credit.

$\bar{e}$ – Maximum exemption.

e_i – Bracket-exemption of the i-th net-income bracket.

$e(Y)$ – Exemption.

$f(Y)$ – Tax liability.

g_i – Upper endpoint of the i-th taxable-income bracket.

$g(Y)$ – Taxable income.

k – Rate of decline of the exemption.

$R = f(Y)$ – See $f(Y)$.

$\bar{r}$ – Proportional tax rate.

$r(g)$ – Statutory marginal rate for taxable income g.

r_i – Statutory marginal tax rate of the i-th income bracket.

s – Rate of standard deduction.

$V(Y)$ – Absolute tax value of the exemption.

w – Gross marginal rate of remuneration.

w_n – Net marginal rate of remuneration for the n-th income bracket.

X – Disposable income.

Y – Net income.

Y_i – Upper endpoint of the i-th net-income bracket.

SELECTED BIBLIOGRAPHY

Public Documents

U.S. *Internal Revenue Code*. 1954 Code Edition. Chicago, New York, Washington: Commerce Clearing House, Inc., 1954.

U.S. Staff of the Joint Committee on Internal Revenue Taxation. *Alternative Plans for Reducing the Individual Income Tax Burden*. Washington: Government Printing Office, 1956.

U.S. Treasury Department, Division of Tax Research. *Individual Income Tax Exemptions*. Washington: Government Printing Office, 1947.

U.S. Treasury Department, Internal Revenue Service. *Statistics of Income for 1951*. Washington: Government Printing Office, 1955.

Books

BLACK, DUNCAN. *The Incidence of Income Taxes*. London: Macmillan & Co., Ltd., 1939.

BLUM, WALTER J. AND KALVEN JR., HARRY. *The Uneasy Case for Progressive Taxation*. Chicago: University of Chicago Press, 1953.

BRÄUER, KARL. *Umrisse und Untersuchungen zu einer Lehre vom Steuertarif*. Jena: Gustav Fischer, 1927.

FOLLIET, PIERRE. *Les Tarifs d'Impôts; Essai de Mathématiques Fiscales*. Lausanne: Librairie Payot, 1947.

HICKS, JOHN. R. *Value and Capital*. 2nd ed.; Oxford: Clarendon Press, 1946.

MARSHALL, ALFRED. *Principles of Economics*. 8th ed.; London: Macmillan & Co., Ltd., 1920.

MERING, OTTO VON. *The Shifting and Incidence of Taxation*. Philadelphia: The Blakiston Co., 1942.

MUSGRAVE, RICHARD A. *The Theory of Public Finance*. New York, Toronto, London: McGraw-Hill Book Co., Inc., 1959.

Pigou, Arthur C. *A Study in Public Finance*. 3d ed.; London: Macmillan & Co., Ltd., 1947.

Prentice Hall. *Federal Tax Course 1947–1960*. New York: Prentice Hall Inc., 1946, 1947, 1948, 1949, 1950, 1951, 1952, 1953, 1954, 1955, 1956, 1957, 1958, 1959

Shultz, William J. and Harriss, C. Lowell. *American Public Finance*. 7th ed.; Englewood Cliffs, N. J.: Prentice-Hall, Inc., 1959.

Vickrey, William. *Agenda for Progressive Taxation*. New York: The Ronald Press Co., 1947.

Articles

Break, George F. "The Effects of Taxation on Work Incentives," in *Federal Tax Policy for Economic Growth and Stability;* Papers Submitted by Panelists Appearing Before the Subcommittee on Tax Policy. Joint Committee on the Economic Report. Washington: U.S. Government Printing Office, 1956, pp. 192–199.

——. "Income Taxes, Wage Rates, and the Incentive to Supply Labor Services," *National Tax Journal*, VI (December, 1953), pp. 333–352.

Cooper, Gershon. "Taxation and Incentive in Mobilization," *Quarterly Journal of Economics*, LXVI (February, 1952), pp. 43–66.

Edgeworth, Francis Y. "The Pure Theory of Taxation," in *Papers Relating to Political Economy*. London: Macmillan & Co., Ltd., 1925, II, pp. 63–125.

Gerloff, Wilhelm. "Steuerwirtschaftslehre," in *Handbuch der Finanzwissenschaft*, II. 2nd ed.; Tübingen: J. C. B. Mohr (Paul Siebeck), 1956, pp. 239–325.

Goode, Richard. "The Income Tax and the Supply of Labor," *Journal of Political Economy*, LVII (October, 1949), pp. 428–437.

Hicks, John R. and Allen, R. G. D. "A Reconsideration of the Theory of Value," *Economica*, New Series, 1 (February, 1934), pp. 52–76; 2 (May, 1934), pp. 196–219.

Laufenburger, Henry. "Die Einkommensbesteuerung," in *Handbuch der Finanzwissenschaft*, II. 2nd ed.; Tübingen: J. C. B. Mohr (Paul Siebeck), 1956, pp. 447–501.

Long, Clarence D. "Impact of the Federal Income Tax on Labor Force

Participation," in *Federal Tax Policy for Economic Growth and Stability;* Papers Submitted by Panelists Appearing Before the Subcommittee on Tax Policy. Joint Committee on the Economic Report. Washington: U.S. Government Printing Office, 1956, pp. 153–166.

MUSGRAVE, RICHARD A. AND THIN, TUN. "Income Tax Progression, 1929–48," *Journal of Political Economy,* LVI (December, 1948), pp. 498–514.

PREINREICH, G. A. D. "Progressive Taxation and Sacrifice," *American Economic Review,* XXXVIII (March, 1948), pp. 103–117.

ROBBINS, LIONEL. "On the Elasticity of Demand for Income in Terms of Effort," *Economica,* X (June, 1930), pp. 123–129. reprinted in *Readings in the Theory of Income Distribution;* Philadelphia: The Blakiston Co., 1949, pp. 237–244.

SHOUP, CARL S. "Taxation and Fiscal Policy," in *Income Stabilization for a Developing Democracy.* Ed. Max Millikan. New Haven: Yale University Press, 1953, pp. 261–302.

VICKREY, WILLIAM. "Adjustment of Income Tax Schedules for Small Incomes," in *Federal Tax Policy for Economic Growth and Stability;* Papers Submitted by Panelists Appearing Before the Subcommittee on Tax Policy. Joint Committee on the Economic Report. Washington: U.S. Government Printing Office, 1956, pp. 347–353.

—. "Rate Reduction or Increased Exemptions: The Economics of the Question," *National Tax Association.* 1954 Proceedings of the Forty-Seventh Annual Conference on Taxation. Sacramento: 1955, pp. 288–295.

—. "Some Limits to the Income Elasticity of Income Tax Yields," *Review of Economics and Statistics,* XXXI (May, 1949), pp. 140–144.

WALD, HASKELL P. "The Classical Indictment of Indirect Taxation," *Quarterly Journal of Economics,* LIX (August, 1945), pp. 577–596.

INDEX

Ability to pay, 9–10

Absolute tax value: Of exemption, 2, 27–28 (defined), 31; under progressive taxation, 41–43, 117, 121, 134, 137; under proportional taxation, 27–29, 31, 130; of standard deduction, 119–121, 141; of tax credit, 114–115

Administrative considerations: Of carry-over of exemption, 26; of statutory revenue changes, 70, 110–112

Allen, R. G. D., 74 fn., 144

Average-rate progression (ARP): And standard deduction, 119–123; and tax credit, 115–117, 140; as a basic measure of tax progressivity, 37–39; under progressive taxation, 50–51, 54, 60–62, 64–68, 70–73, 135–136; under proportional taxation, 30, 32 (defined)–36, 130–131

Averaging: And tax criterion IV, 25; of income, 11 fn.; of exemptions, 25–26

Black, Duncan, 73 fn., 74 fn., 75 fn., 143

Blum, Walter J., 143

Bracket-exemptions, 52 (defined)–62, 64–67, 133–136

Bräuer, Karl, 2, 5 fn., 17 fn., 18 fn., 88 fn., 143

Break, George F., 73 fn., 75 fn., 144

Burns, Arthur F., v.

Carry-over: Loss, 11; of exemptions, 26

Changes in tax parameters: Under progressive taxation, 61–112, 135–137; under proportional taxation, 27, 33–36, 131

Continuing exemption, *see* exemptions, continuing

Cooper, Gershon, 73 fn., 75 fn., 144

Countercyclical effects: Carry-back of unused exemptions, 26; linking exemptions to Consumer Price Index, 112 fn.

Coverage of income-tax payers, 69–72, 111

Dopsch, 12 fn.

Edgeworth, Francis Y., 16 fn., 144

Effective marginal rate, 15 (defined), 22–23, 42, 128

Equalizing ratios of $\varepsilon/\varepsilon_p$, 102–104

Exemptions: And size of family, 116–118; changes in size of, 27, 34–36, 61–63, 69–73, 81–95, 104–112, 137; range of decline of, 7–9, 22–24, 28–29, 33–35, 128–129; rate of decline of, 2, 7–9, 22–24, 27–28, 33–34

Exemptions, bracket-, *see* bracket-exemptions

Exemptions, continuing: Absolute tax value of, 2, 28–29, 31, 41–43, 134; and progressivity under progressive taxation, 50–51, 61–63, 71–72, 135–136; and progressivity under proportional taxation, 31–32; and tax criteria, 25, 128; changes in size of, 61–63, 69–73, 81–95, 104–112; defined, 6, 127; in relation to linearly declining exemption,